Photographs by Alan Wycheck

STACKPOLE
BOOKS

Published by
STACKPOLE BOOKS
5067 Ritter Road
Mechanicsburg, PA 17055
www.stackpolebooks.com

Printed in China

10 9 8 7 6 5 4 3 2 1

First edition

Cover design by Tessa J. Sweigert

Library of Congress Cataloging-in-Publication Data

Johnston, Michael, 1947–
Making stained glass boxes / Michael Johnston ; photographs by Alan Wycheck. — 1st ed.
p. cm.
ISBN-13: 978-0-8117-3594-0
ISBN-10: 0-8117-3594-X
1. Glass craft. 2. Box making. I. Title.
TT298.J65 2009
748.5—dc22

2008049634

contents

acknowledgments

This project is dedicated to our family matriarch, Angela Patterson Johnston. Your pretty colors have rubbed off onto all of us.

As the process for *Making Stained Glass Boxes* began to unfold, it soon became obvious that many people would have an important hand in its development.

Foremost, I thank Mark Allison from Stackpole Books for his patience and expert guidance from the conceptualization of the project clear through to the final product.

Thanks also to photographer extraordinaire Alan Wycheck. He has a keen ability to see things most people miss and then capture them with his Nikon.

Much appreciation goes out to my loyal Rainbowers: Lynn Haunstein, Nan Maund, and Lee Summer. In addition to contributing designs and samples for the Stained Glass Box Gallery, they all ably assisted in many aspects of the book's production.

Melissa Flood, my older daughter, accurately interpreted my chicken scratch and was able to get everything into the computer. Ashley Johnston, my younger daughter, utilized skills learned in her honors English course and provided a comprehensive first-round editing. Craig Johnston, my firstborn, was instrumental in coaching me through some of the complicated times. Because of the three of them, I consider myself a very fortunate father.

Last, I thank Jane, my chief promoter and wife of twenty-five years. Her encouragement and assistance, as well as her willingness to forego lots of family time, made this possible. She's the best.

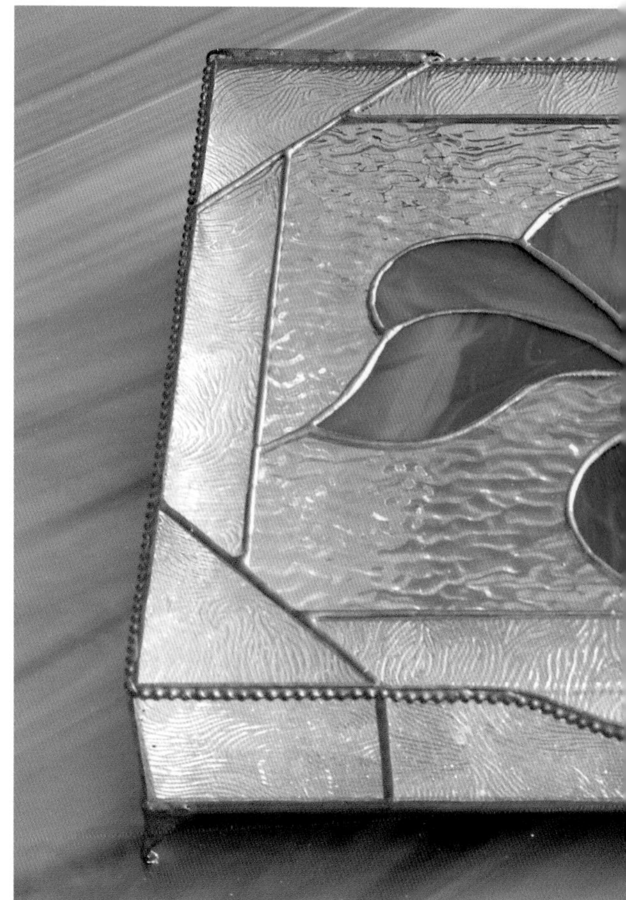

introduction

A colorful stained glass box can be a wonderful complement to any home decor while it safeguards treasures, keepsakes, jewelry, and more. In this book, we have detailed all the steps for making an elaborate glass jewelry box.

Three-dimensional items generally require some previous experience, particularly in the basic skills of cutting and soldering. Because of this prerequisite, we have included teaching primers in both areas in order to prepare you for the successful completion of your box.

Even though you might feel skilled in the craft and do not anticipate any problems with box making, you might want to work through the cutting and soldering techniques prior to starting your box. We hope that you will pick up, at minimum, a few useful ideas.

Once the primers are completed to your satisfaction, you can then move on to the specifics of box construction. You will learn to square up the box sides, install braces and an inside shelf, hinge the box lid, attach a safety chain, and secure box feet. You will also become acquainted with advanced cutting and soldering techniques as well as how to care for a mirror and, just in case, how to repair broken glass.

While all of the procedures in the book are intended as steps in making the featured box design, you will be able to apply these skills to boxes of various sizes and shapes with any alternate lid designs you choose. This project is not particularly easy, so with its successful completion, you will have attained a reasonable level of stained glass skill.

In addition to average hand dexterity, you should plan to bring one other skill to the project: patience. Take your time; read all instruction details; be as precise as possible. If you are patient, you will be well on your way to completing a beautiful jewelry box.

Now, let's get started.

1 A Good Work Environment

AS YOUR INTEREST IN STAINED GLASS BLOSSOMS, you will discover that you are spending a great deal of time in your glass shop. You will want some creature comforts. Four elements greatly contribute to a comfortable and efficient shop:

- good light source
- sturdy work table
- nearby water source
- adequate ventilation

All aspects of stained glass making (cutting, foiling, soldering, and so on) involve a need for precision, and the better you see, the better the final product will be. A two- or four-bulb fluorescent light hanging over a workbench is generally adequate.

A work table should be sturdy and at a height comfortable for the user. If you are of average height, a tabletop approximately 34 inches from the floor will probably work well. Plywood construction is ideal, and a size of 30 inches by 72 inches will handle most projects. The gray-colored work surface shown here is a piece of fire-resistant Homasote about 2 feet by 3 feet in size that can be placed on the plywood.

Homasote has a firm surface with a slight spring, which makes it perfect for glass cutting. (Plywood by itself is a bit rigid.) Pins and nails are easily secured in Homasote, and soldering is easier and safer due to its fire resistance. Homasote used to be readily available at all building supply stores but is no longer as common. You might have to call around to find it or settle for a substitute product.

In addition to providing the crafter with a handy place to wash up, a nearby sink will make it easy to clean the project at several stages. Any size basin can work, but one with an opening 12 inches by 20 inches or larger is ideal. Plan to use a screen strainer to prevent sand and other debris from making their way into your drainpipes.

Set up a shop in the area that is convenient to you based on what rooms you have available. You will only have so many options, so you'll need to do the best you can with your space. Ideally, you will want a room with good ventilation so air can move through your work area during the soldering stage. If this type of setup is not possible, use a small table fan on your work table or purchase a smoke absorber, which is available at stained glass supply stores. You can also experiment with opening adjacent doors and windows to create a cross breeze in your work area.

In addition to the shop features listed on page 1, several other items will be very useful:

- bench brush and dustpan, for cleaning up glass shards and other debris
- storage bins for sheets of glass
- cabinet for chemicals and tools
- comfortable stool
- radio or CD or MP3 player
- multi-receptacle surge suppressor with LED light for operating several electrical items plugged in at once (the light will act as a visual reminder to turn off your soldering iron at the end of each work session).

STAINED GLASS SAFETY

Making stained glass is generally a very safe craft, and by adopting the safety precautions listed here, you will greatly reduce the likelihood of injuries and health problems.

- The most common injury that occurs in crafting stained glass is a cut finger. Prevention includes careful handling of the glass and frequent sweeping of your work area to eliminate shards and specks of glass.
- If you do get a cut, tend to it immediately by applying an antiseptic and adhesive bandage. Keep these items at close hand in your shop.

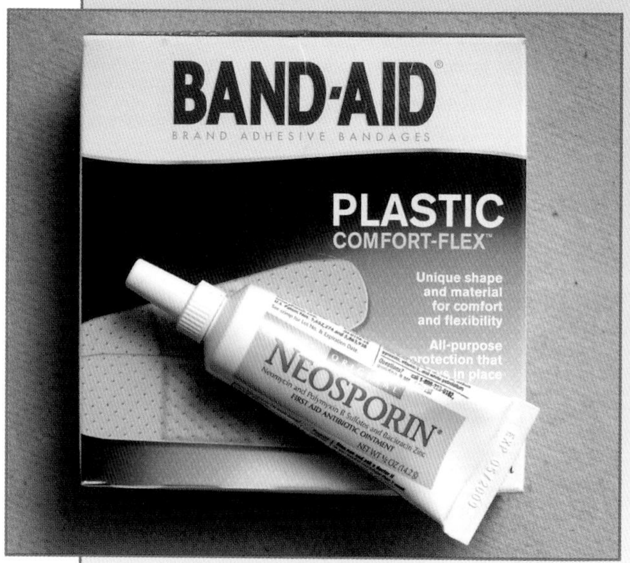

- Never eat, drink, or smoke while engaged in any of the steps in making stained glass items.

- Be careful and use common sense when working with lead cames and solder. Generally, stained glass crafters are exposed to only very low levels of lead while building their projects. Make sure to bandage any open wounds and thoroughly wash your hands after working with lead or solder.
- Wear closed-toed shoes at all times to avoid glass injuries to your feet.
- Do not allow children or pets in your work area.
- Use rubber gloves when working with patinas and etching cream. These substances can cause chemical burns on exposed skin and be harmful if absorbed into the bloodstream.
- Always wear safety glasses when cutting or grinding glass.
- Use care when handling large sheets of glass. Grip the sheet by its top edge and move it slowly to avoid jarring. Never hold a large sheet of glass horizontally because it might crack from the strain. Never try to catch a falling sheet of glass—let it go and move quickly out of the way.
- To avoid burns, use a heavy-duty stand to house your soldering iron when not in use.
- Take care that the cord of the soldering iron does not become entangled in the spirals of the stand; otherwise, the cord may be damaged and electrical problems may occur.
- When soldering, position your head so that you are not directly breathing in fumes from the flux.
- Always wash your hands thoroughly after working in any phase of stained glass construction.
- Avoid soldering in tight spaces with little ventilation. Create airflow with a small fan or open windows. Smoke absorbers (shown below) are also available in most stained glass supply shops.

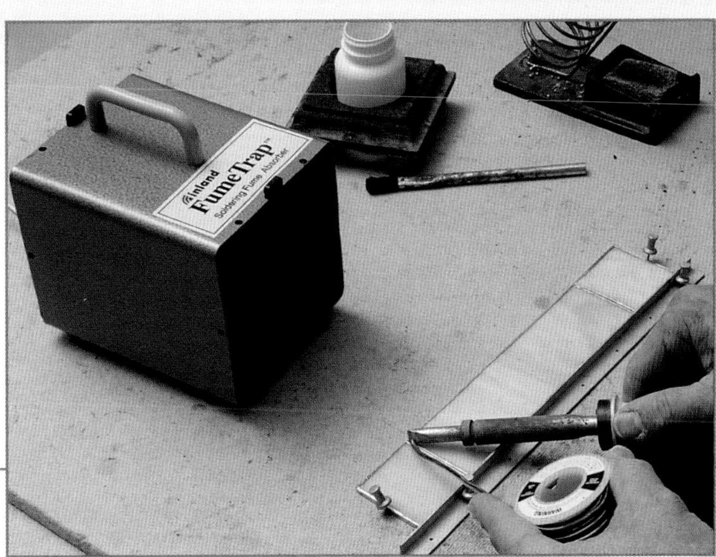

2

Equipment and Materials

IF YOU HAVE BEEN WORKING WITH STAINED glass, you probably have most of the tools necessary to complete a glass box. If you are just now exploring the craft and are ready to purchase equipment, the following information is intended as a helpful guide.

The three most important tools you will use include a glass cutter, breaking/grozing pliers, and a soldering iron. If you envision doing additional stained glass projects, and your budget allows, plan to buy quality versions of these tools. Not only will you become more glass proficient, but quality tools will also typically last much longer than cheaper models.

All the tools, equipment, and materials used to make a glass box are listed on the following pages; a checklist appears at the end of the chapter. Bear in mind that many different brands of similar items are available, so if you have access to a stained glass supply store, get to know the proprietor. He or she will be able to advise you as you begin to develop your tool arsenal.

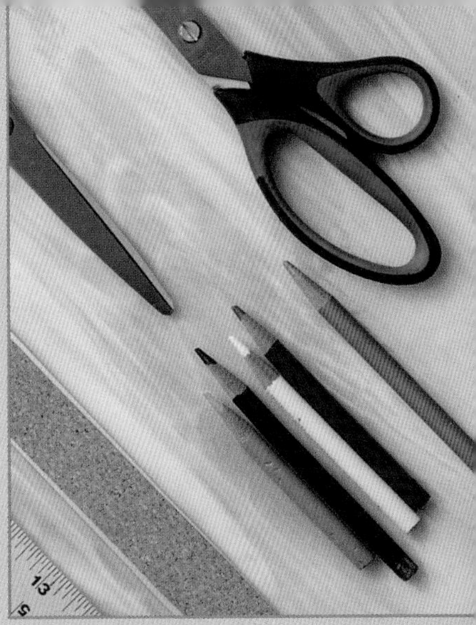

- **Tracing paper.** Thin, white translucent paper; allows lines from the original pattern to show through for tracing.
- **Carbon paper.** Also called transfer paper; inky paper transfers the pattern from the white paper to the oak tag.
- **Oak tag.** Has a thickness similar to a manila file folder; used for laying out the glass once it has been cut and ground.
- **Masking tape and writing implements.**

- **Cork-backed ruler.** Used for cutting straight edges and measuring; cork helps to prevent the ruler from slipping on smooth glass.
- **Rubber cement.** Used for temporarily attaching paper patterns to glass.
- **Pattern shears.** Special three-bladed shears that remove a thin strip of the paper pattern; reduces each pattern piece just enough so that when copper foil is applied to the project, the pattern returns to its original size.
- **Household scissors.** Used for trimming foil and paper patterns.
- **Colored pencils.** For assigning color designations to each paper pattern piece.

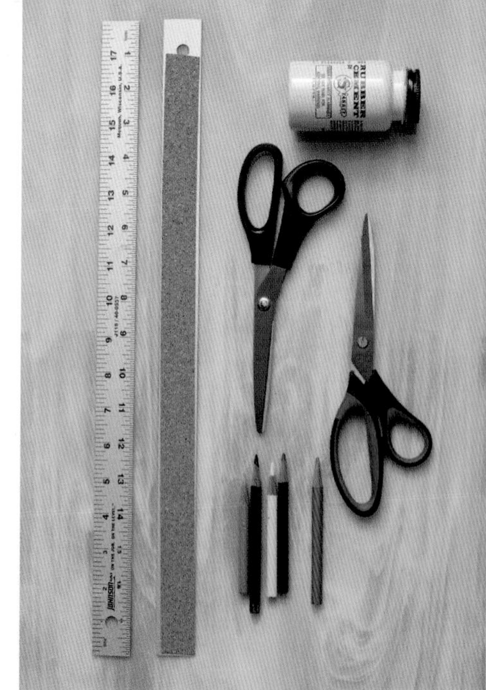

- **Pistol grip cutter.** Variation on the upright cutter that allows you to use the bigger muscles in your hand, resulting in less hand fatigue or cramping; a spring in the tip activates the oil, and the head swivels for ease in cutting curves.
- **Upright steel wheel cutter.** The least expensive of the glass cutters; notches can be used to break off pieces of glass, and the ball on the top is used to run a score line after the initial scoring.
- **Upright pencil-shaped cutter.** Features an oil-fed carbide cutting wheel with an acrylic barrel; cutting lubricant is added through a small hole at the top of the handle.

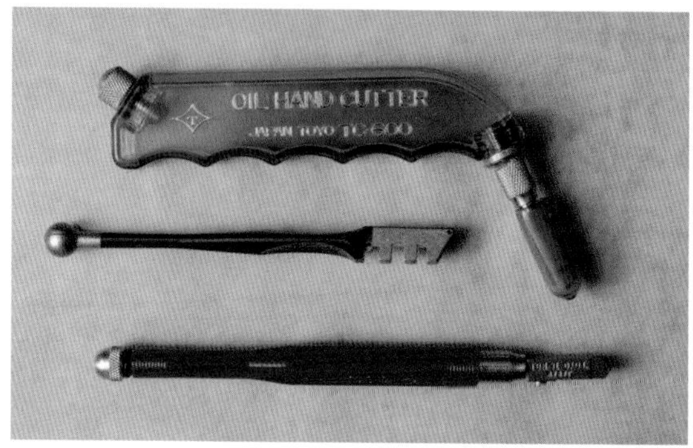

- **Cutting square.** Has a ridge on both sides of the shorter leg; when placed on a straight edge of glass, it indicates a perfect 90-degree angle; used for squaring irregular edges and cutting strips.
- **Thumb square.** Small square used for cutting sections from glass strips.
- **Running pliers.** Used for breaking glass once it has been scored; the upper jaw has a node on each side, while the lower jaw has a node in the middle. After the white indicator line is placed on a score line, a light squeeze will separate the glass.
- **Breaking/grozing pliers** (shown above). Used to break off excess glass after a score and for grozing—nibbling off pieces of excess glass that cannot be removed by cutting and breaking.

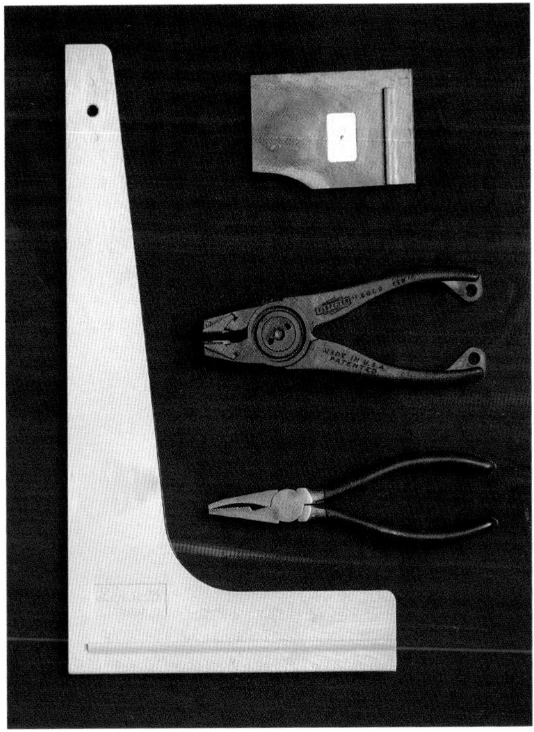

- **Homasote board.** Compressed fiberboard that has a firm surface with a slight spring, making it ideal for cutting glass; fire resistant; allows liquids to bead up; pushpins and tacks are easily inserted and removed.
- **Mirror protector.** A chemical that seals the back of mirrored glass; prevents flux and patina from eroding the silvering on the mirror, which could result in a visible deterioration of the surface.

- **Bench brush.** Used to sweep shards of glass and bits of solder from the work surface.
- **Safety glasses.** Used for eye protection during several steps in the stained glass building process.
- **Glass grinder.** Machine that smoothes rough edges of glass pieces that have been cut and grozed; a diamond bit immersed in water safely removes excess glass in seconds.
- **Grinder coolant.** A concentrate added to the water in the grinder's chassis to extend the

life of the grinding bit by reducing friction; lubricates the chassis, making cleanup a breeze.

- **Glass markers.** Used for writing or drawing on glass; can be removed with soap and water.
- **Carborundum stone.** Metal abrasive stone that will take off sharp edges or burrs from glass.

- **Foiling machine.** Comes with sizing wheels for the three most common foil widths ($^{3}/_{16}$, $^{7}/_{32}$, and $^{1}/_{4}$); allows each glass piece to be centered on the foil and applies the foil evenly, saving lots of time.

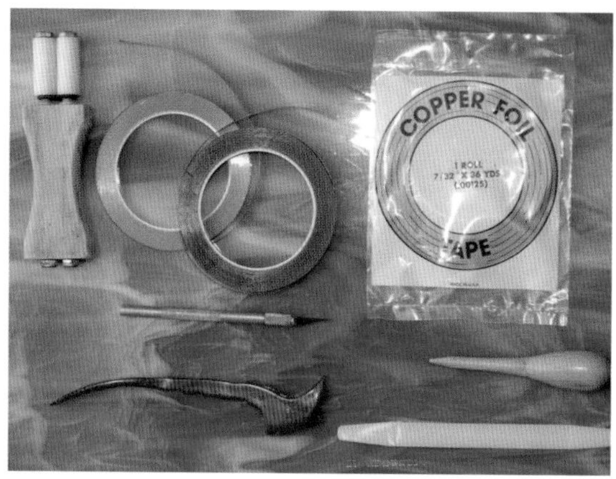

- **Fids.** Come in assorted styles and shapes; used to burnish foil to the glass after it has been applied and folded down.
- **Craft knife.** Used to trim uneven edges of foil.
- **Foil finisher.** Tool that allows for the burnishing of foil on both edges of the glass at once; glass slides between the two plastic rollers that are under tension.
- **Copper foil.** Available in 36-yard rolls with various widths, thicknesses, and color backings; foil is backed with adhesive, allowing it to be attached to glass.

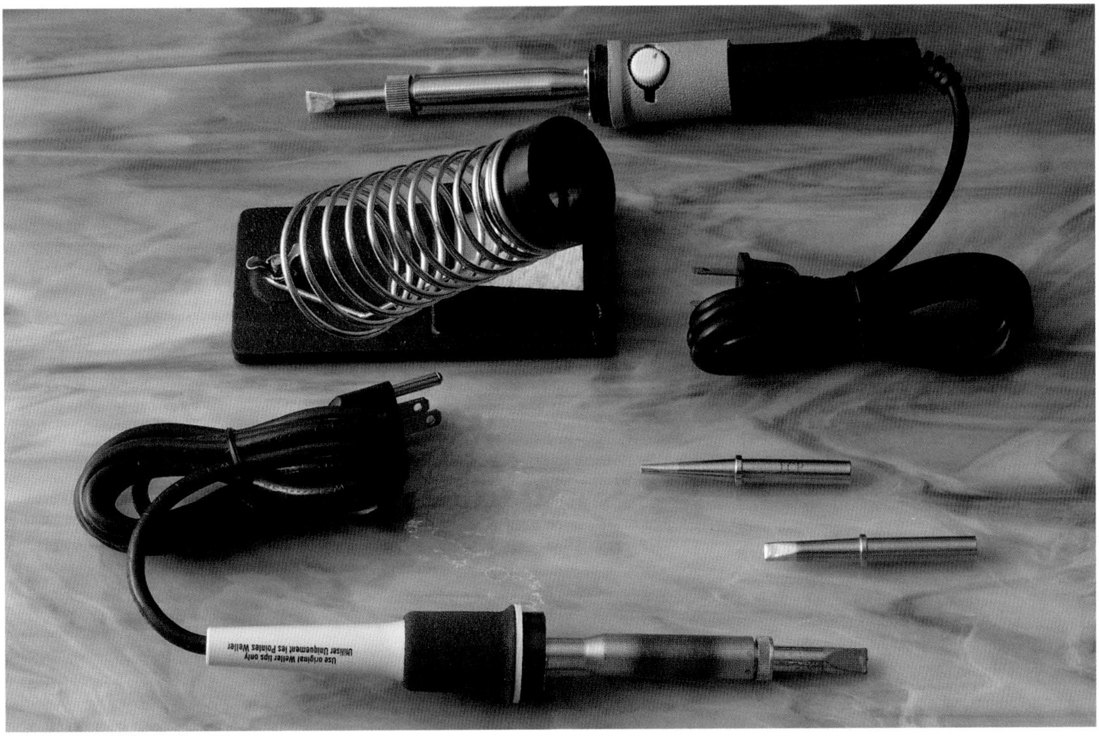

- **Soldering iron.** Tool that melts solder onto the copper foil seams. Three features should be considered when choosing an iron: wattage (80 to 100 watts is usually fine), a way to control the temperature, and a chisel-shaped tip (1/4 to 3/8 inch wide is recommended for general work).
- **Soldering iron stand.** Tool that houses the iron; should be sturdy enough to hold it upright; typically has a tray in front for a sponge that is used to clean the iron's tip.
- **Soldering iron tips.** Come in different widths; 1/4 to 3/8 inch is standard.
- **Layout block.** Aluminum bars of various lengths used to square up and hold projects in place prior to soldering; pushpins secure the strips to a work surface.
- **Solder.** A tin/lead alloy melted onto foil seams that connect the glass pieces in a project; 60/40 solder (60 percent tin and 40 percent lead) is standard.

- **Flux.** A chemical used to deoxidize copper foil so solder flows smoothly and attaches well; liquid or gel fluxes are generally used on copper foil and are applied with a small brush.

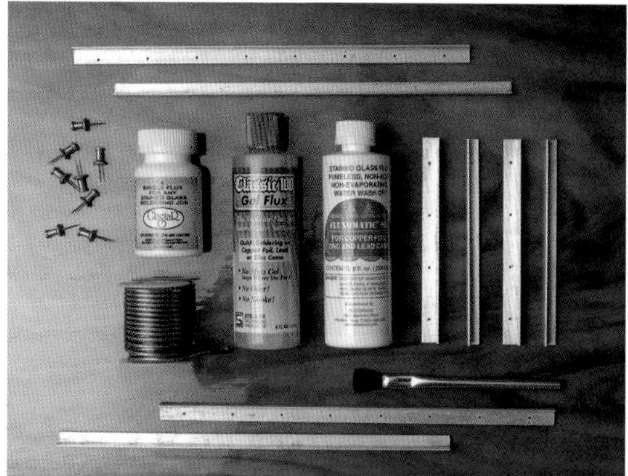

- **Block glass holders.** Wooden blocks are great aides for soldering the edges of glass; sizes vary (ours are 2 inches by 4 inches by 6 inches with $^{3}/_{16}$-inch notches cut at one end and side); a woodworking neighbor can make a pair from an old 2 by 4.

- **Box chain.** Decorative chain used as a safety feature to allow a box lid to stay open on its own; available in many colors.
- **Brass tube and rod.** Make up the hinges of a box; the smaller rod goes inside the larger tube.
- **Needle-nose pliers.** Used to hold metal items in place, such as chains and tubes, while they are being soldered.
- **Wire cutters.** Used to cut wire and chain.
- **Utility knife.** Used to put a score line on a brass tube prior to breaking it. A small metal file can be used for this, too.
- **Tube cutter.** An alternative tool used to cut a metal tube.

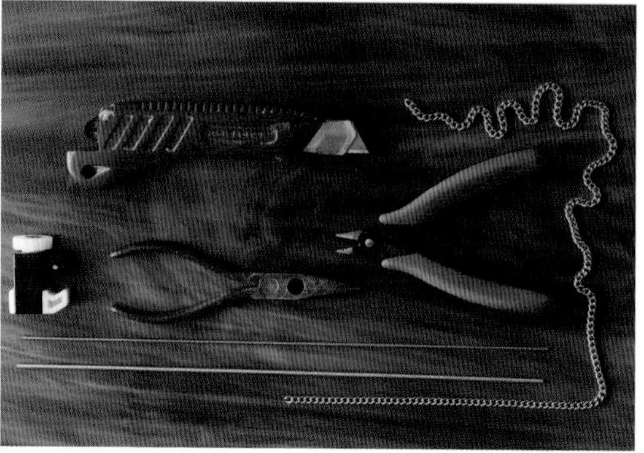

- **Finishing wax.** A chemical polish that puts a protective coating and shine on the finished project.
- **Flux remover.** Neutralizes and removes flux and patina; use before applying patina and before the final waxing.
- **Patina.** Chemicals that oxidize on solder in various colors; black and copper are most common; apply with a soft sponge.

CHECKLIST: BUILDING A STAINED GLASS BOX ✔

Tools

- ☐ Soldering Iron
- ☐ Iron Stand
- ☐ 1/8-inch Iron Tip
- ☐ Breaking/Grozing Pliers
- ☐ Grinder
- ☐ Carborundum Stone
- ☐ Pattern Shears
- ☐ Glass Square
- ☐ Thumb Square
- ☐ Glass Cutter
- ☐ Running Pliers
- ☐ Foiling Machine
- ☐ Foil Finisher
- ☐ Fids
- ☐ Craft Knife
- ☐ Utility Knife
- ☐ Needle-nose Pliers
- ☐ Wire Cutters
- ☐ Metal File
- ☐ Flux Brush

Chemicals

- ☐ Flux
- ☐ Mirror Protector
- ☐ Flux Remover
- ☐ Patina
- ☐ Finishing Compound
- ☐ Rubber Cement
- ☐ Cutter Oil

Supplies

- ☐ 60/40 Solder
- ☐ 7/32-inch Copper Foil
- ☐ Tracing Paper
- ☐ Carbon Paper
- ☐ Oak Tag
- ☐ Masking Tape
- ☐ Box Chain
- ☐ Soft Sponge
- ☐ Window Glass
- ☐ 3/32-inch Brass Tube
- ☐ 1/16-inch Brass Rod
- ☐ Assorted Stained Glass

Miscellaneous

- ☐ Wood Blocks
- ☐ Scissors
- ☐ Layout Strips/Pushpins
- ☐ Ruler
- ☐ Colored Pencils
- ☐ Homasote Board
- ☐ Safety Glasses
- ☐ Markers
- ☐ Sponges
- ☐ Towels
- ☐ Mild Detergent

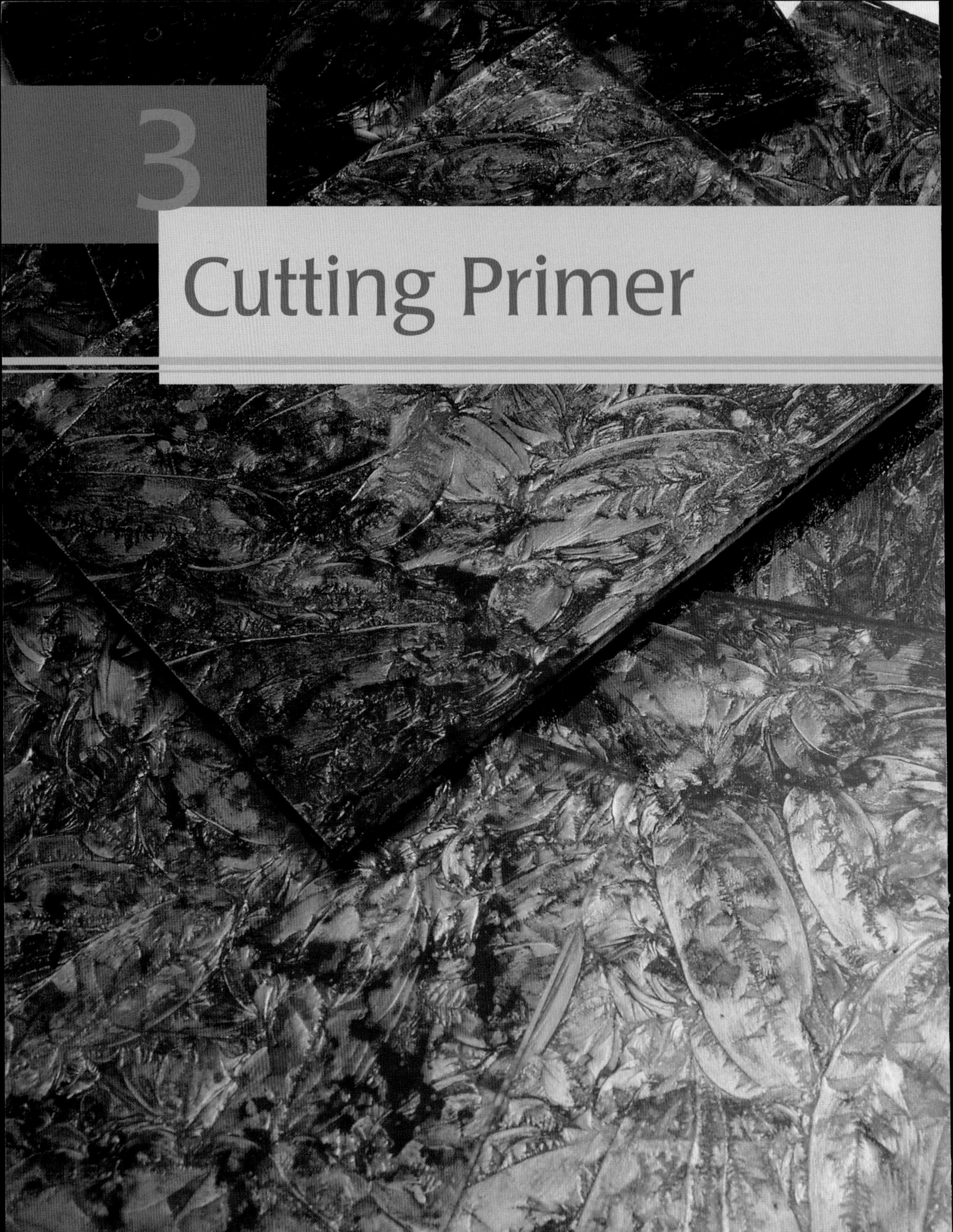

3 Cutting Primer

THE MORE ACCURATELY YOU ARE ABLE TO CUT the glass, the less grozing, grinding, and fitting you will have to do and, ultimately, the nicer the finished product will be. Although glass grinders allow you to fashion a circle from a square in a minute or two, these types of shortcuts are not what the craft is all about. As a crafter of stained glass items, you will want to become adept at cutting glass.

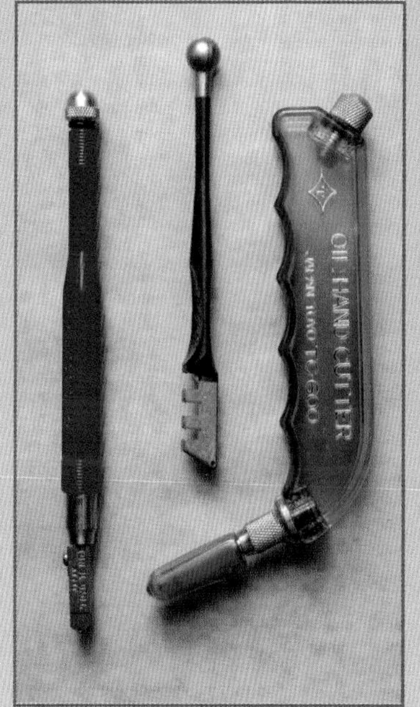

Nearly thirty years have passed since I scored and broke my first sheet of glass, but I have to confess that glass cutting continues to be a pleasure. I still marvel at the way a barely visible scratch in glass can result in a perfectly cut-out shape. And the whole glass experience is so much more enjoyable when the glass actually breaks the way you intend.

Over the past two decades, more than three thousand students have attended our classes, and nearly every student comes in with the idea that glass cutting will be the most difficult of all the related skills. Most new students exhibit some level of trepidation during the early stages of the cutting instruction. Yet after the first two-hour session, most of them begin to feel a confidence in cutting that continues to grow.

The primer that we've included here is intended to allay concerns you might have about glass cutting and get you ready for the successful cutting of your glass box project.

About Cutters

Many different glass cutters are available on the market today, and most can be classified as either upright or pistol shaped. Choose a cutter that is comfortable to use and easy to maneuver. If you see yourself making numerous stained glass items down the road, a cutter is one of three tools on which you should plan to spend some money. Be advised that plenty of budget-priced cutters are available, but our experience has shown that they do not work as well and have a much shorter life than the more expensive cutters. Plan to spend in the $30 to $45 range.

Holding the Cutter

Glass cutters should be held differently, depending on the style you select. The most common cutter is an upright steel wheel cutter with notches and a ball on top, so we'll address that grip first.

1 Start by making a V with the first two fingers of your dominant hand, and slide the cutter between them. Place your index finger in the grip slot in the front and your thumb in the slot in the back. This hand position allows you to steady the cutter.

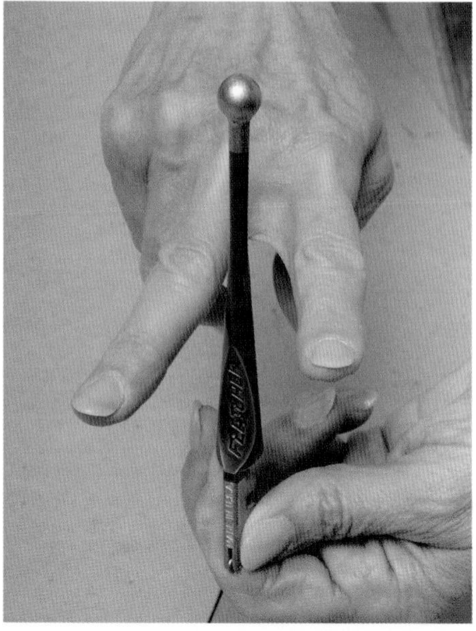

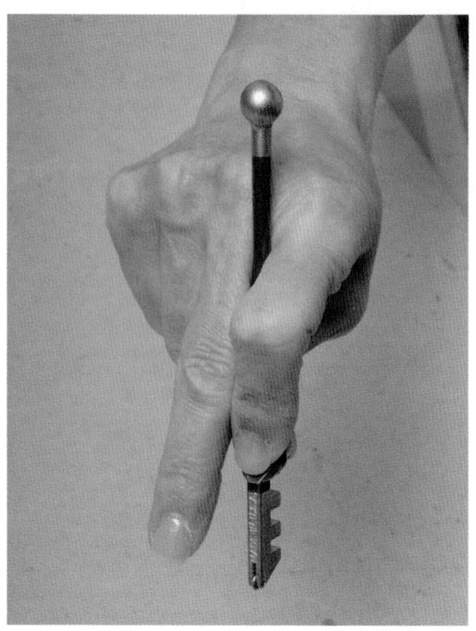

2 Place the thumb from your opposite hand on the ball or top of the cutter and your index finger along the side of the cutter.

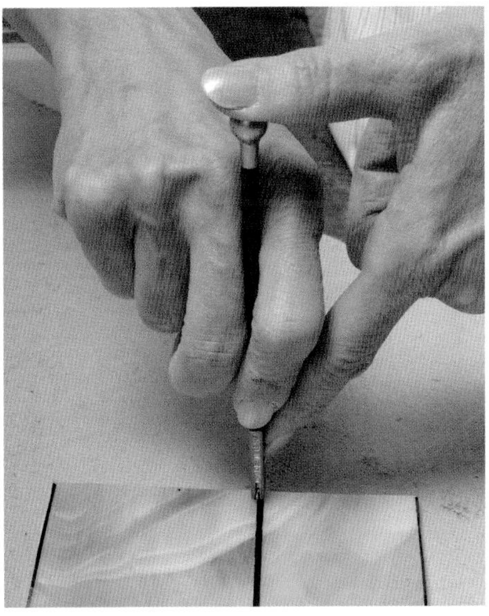

3 As you cut, create pressure on the glass by pushing down with the thumb on the ball; your index finger helps you to guide the cutter. This cutter should be held perpendicular to the glass surface.

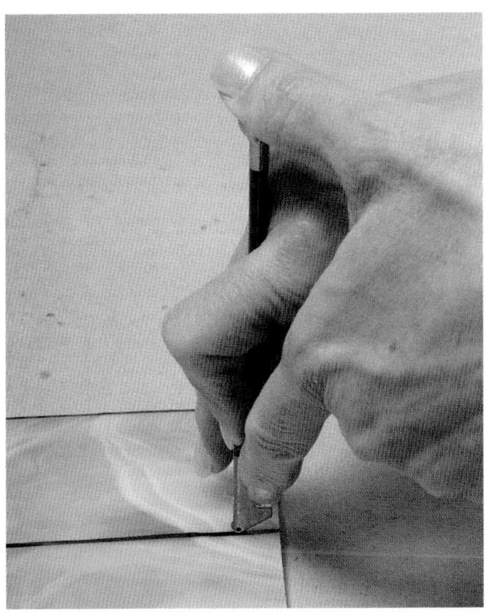

4 An effective grip for an upright pencil-shaped cutter is to hold it like a pencil in your dominant hand.

5 Now overlay this hand with your opposite hand, placing your index finger along the side of the cutter, just off the work surface. This cutter should be tilted back toward you as shown. Apply pressure from the three fingers holding the cylinder in order to score the glass.

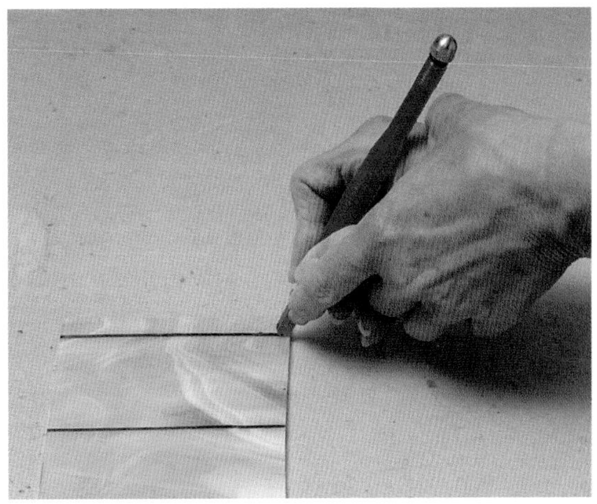

6 If you are using a pistol-shaped cutter, place it in your dominant hand with your thumb on top.

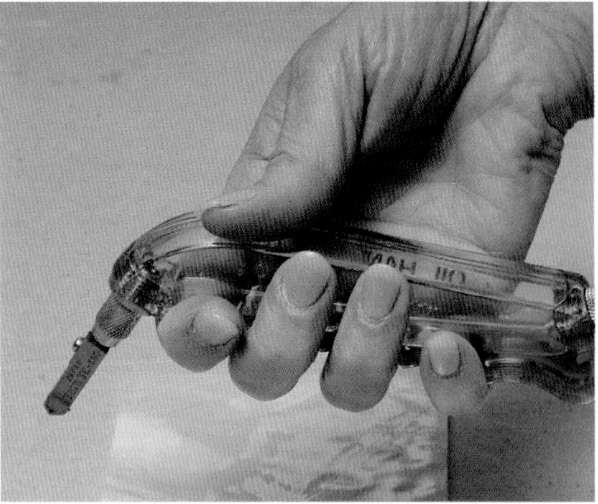

7 Now overlay your other hand on your dominant hand, moving your index finger along the side of the cutter, just off the glass surface.

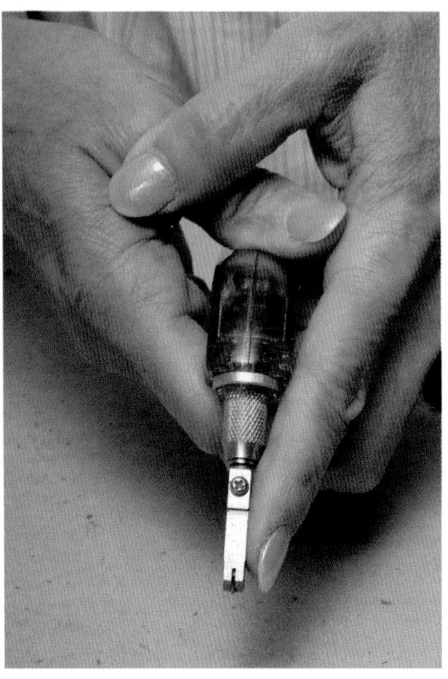

8 The cutter handle should now be parallel to the glass surface with the cutting head angled back slightly.

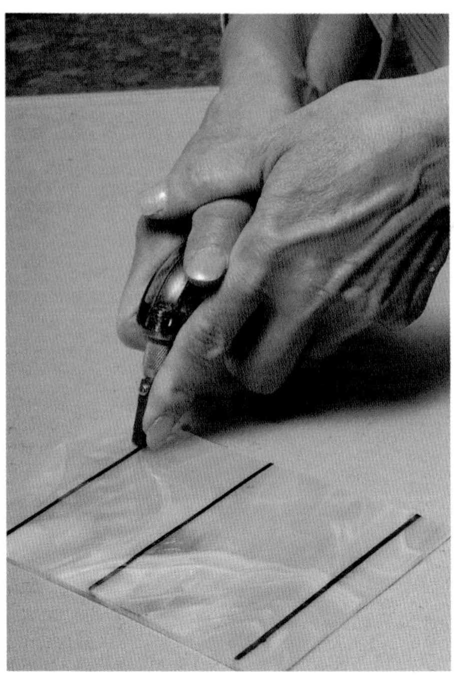

Feeling comfortable with your grip? Probably not, but stick with it—it will get better!

PRO TIP ✔

Cutting oil is used to lubricate the cutting wheel. This keeps the wheel turning freely while reducing friction on the glass. For cutters without oil reservoirs, put a sponge in a baby food jar and saturate with oil. Dip your cutter in the oil every few times you make a score. You can also store your cutter in the jar when not in use.

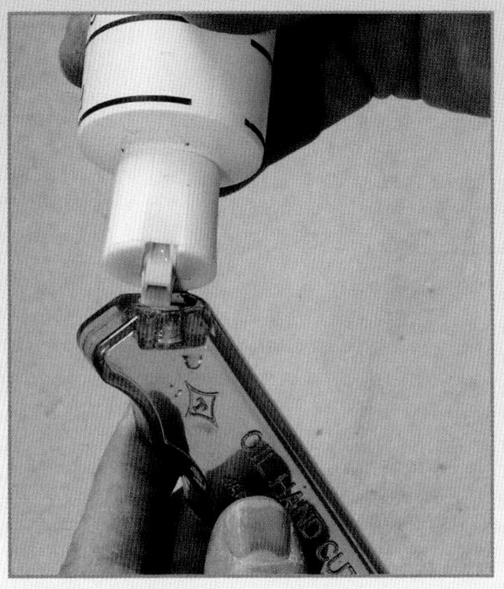

For self-oiling cutters, add oil to approximately 10 percent of capacity. Overfilling leads to leakage, and a little oil lasts a long time. Each day you use your cutter, open the oil reserve hole to allow air to enter. Failure to do this causes a vacuum to form, and oil may not feed onto the wheel.

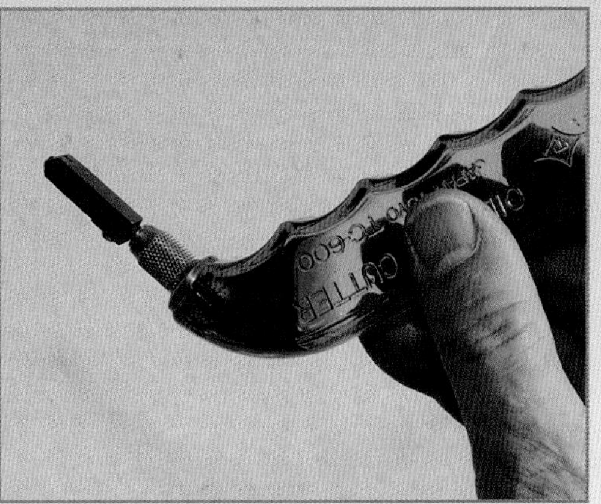

Caution: When replacing the screw, tighten lightly so as not to force the screw into the plastic handle, which could split the seam. This will cause significant and continual leakage.

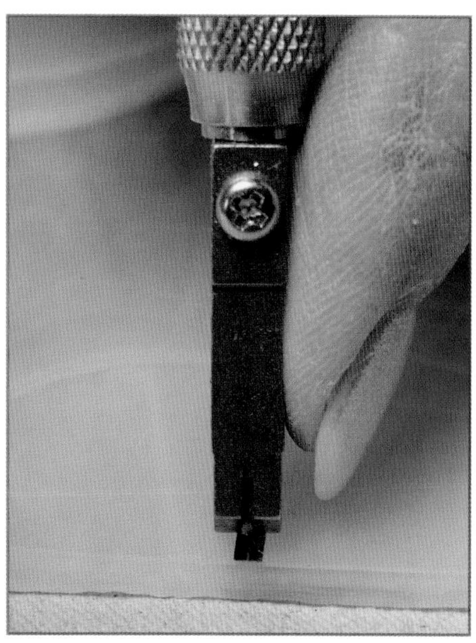

Cutting the Glass

When you begin your cutting practice, you should stand up. You will get better leverage on the cutter by using your large arm and shoulder muscles, and you will be able to see better if you are directly over top of the work.

As you align your cutter on a marker line, you will notice a small slot at the bottom of the cutter; this is exactly where the cutting wheel is located. Starting now and continuing through your entire stained glass career, train your eye to see this groove and line it up exactly with your pattern line during each and every cut.

Now put on your safety glasses and let's do some cutting.

1 On a sheet of glass approximately 4 inches by 6 inches (clear window glass is fine for practice cutting), draw three lines as shown: 1 inch in, 3 inches in, and 3/4 inch from the opposite side.

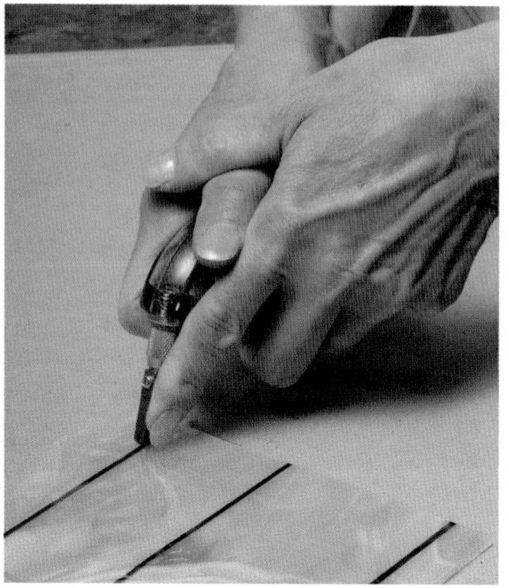

2 Holding the cutter as previously described, start your score 1/16 inch from the edge of the glass closest to you. You should be able to see the cutter's groove on the line during the entire score. Proceed to within 1/16 inch from the opposite edge, attempting to stay on the line the entire time.

3 As you cut, you must put some light pressure on the glass, which will make a slight gritting noise. This is referred to as "scoring." The result is a faint scratch on the glass. Once you've scored the glass, you'll need to finish the break.

Breaking the Glass

You can choose one of three main ways to finish breaking the glass.

Manual break. Place your thumbs parallel to the score line about 1 inch apart. Your index fingers should be bent and curled under the glass as if you were about to snap a cracker in half. Now roll your thumbs outward with that same snapping motion. *Remember to always roll your thumbs outward.*

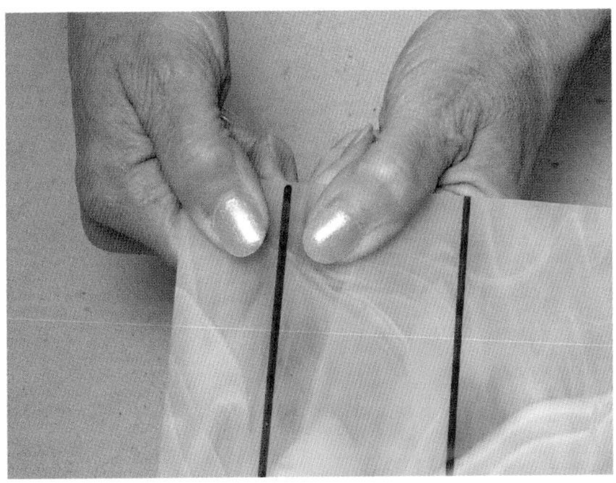

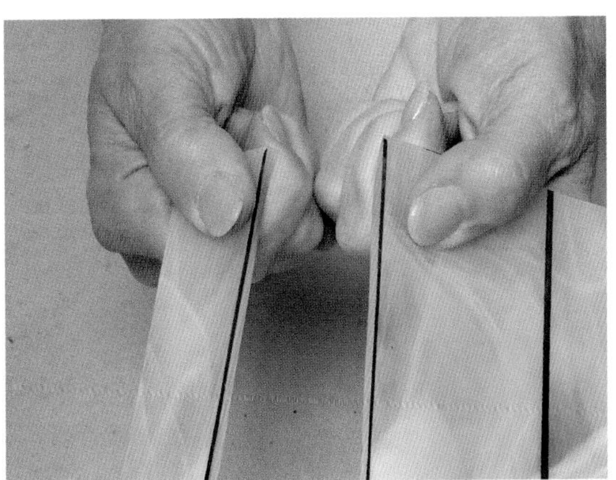

Using breaking pliers. If the scored piece is not wide enough to allow you the leverage to break it off manually, you will need a pair of breaking pliers. Notice that these pliers have a notched upper jaw and curved lower jaw.

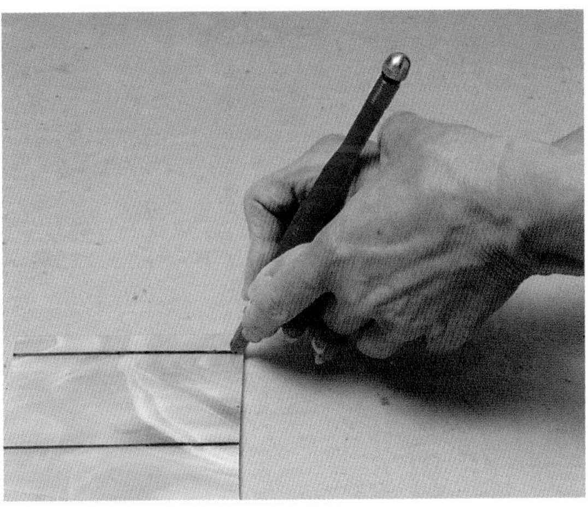

Place these pliers perpendicular to your score line. Be sure the flat tip of the pliers is close to the score line but not on or over the line.

Holding the pliers firmly, snap down using the same outward movement that you used with the manual break. The back of your hand will bend down.

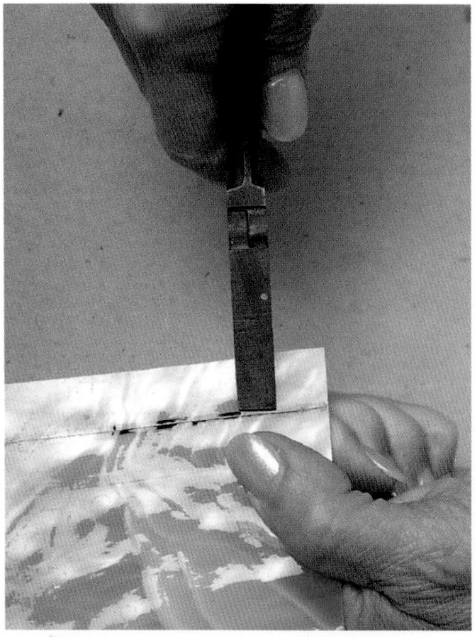

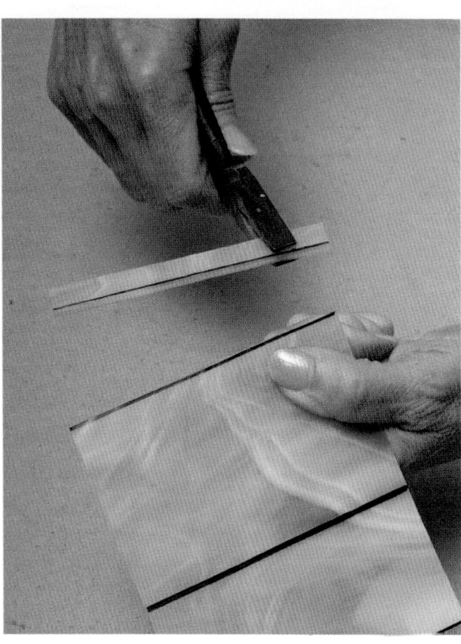

Using running pliers. This tool allows for a more controlled break that starts at the beginning of the score and continues to the end.

Running pliers have two different-shaped jaws and a mark that indicates the top. They must be used in that fashion. Reversing the grip can cause the glass to shatter.

Place the pliers approximately $^1/_4$ inch onto the glass, lining up the indicator line on your pliers with your score line. Squeeze gently to separate the glass.

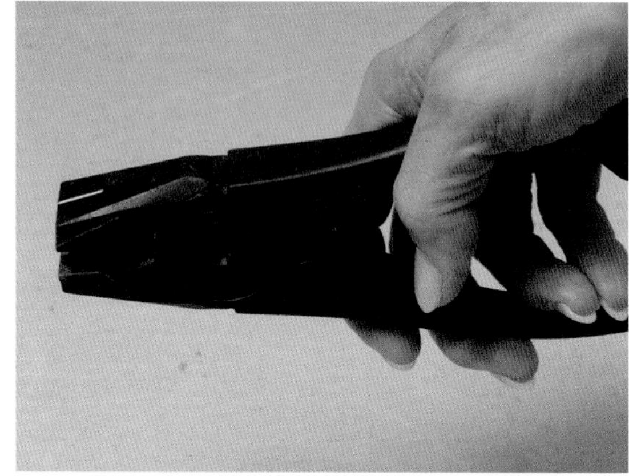

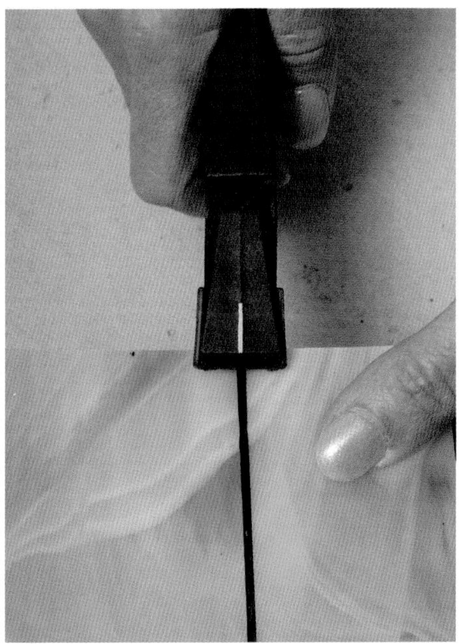

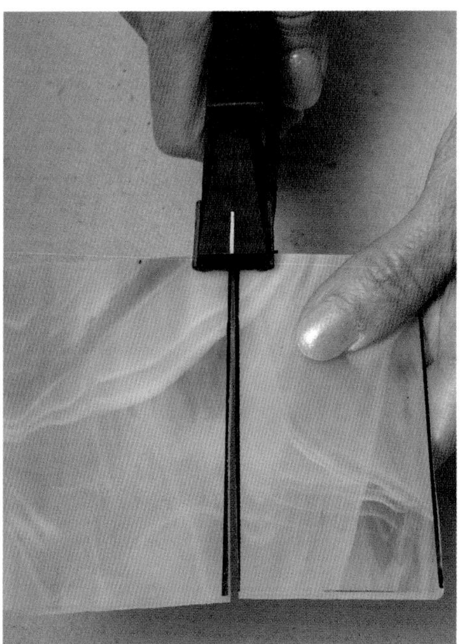

Using another piece of glass, make additional scores and breaks until you are fairly comfortable breaking the glass using the three methods described.

Cutting Shapes with Straight Edges

On a piece of glass approximately 4 inches by 5 inches, draw a version of Practice Piece 1 (see page 23). Starting on the edge closest to you, and remembering to start $^{1}/_{16}$ inch in from the edge, score the glass across to the other side. Remember to stop $^{1}/_{16}$ inch from the edge. Break off the excess glass using any of the three breaking methods .

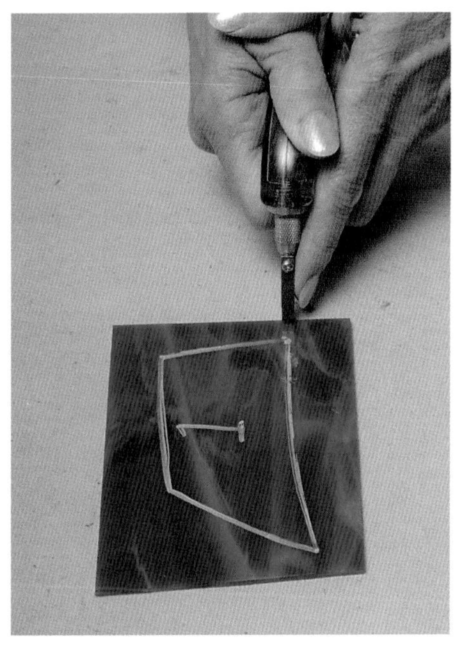

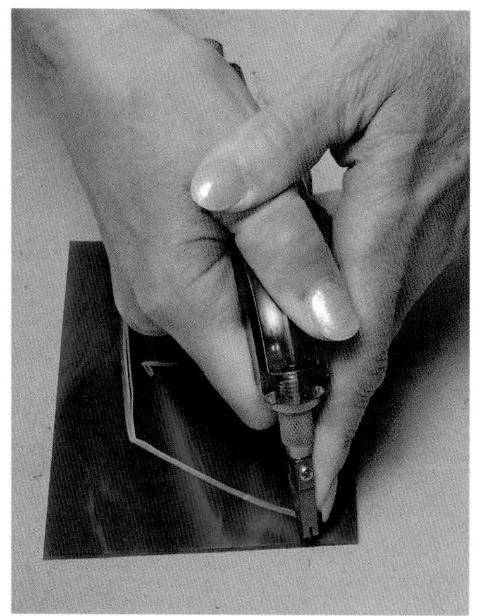

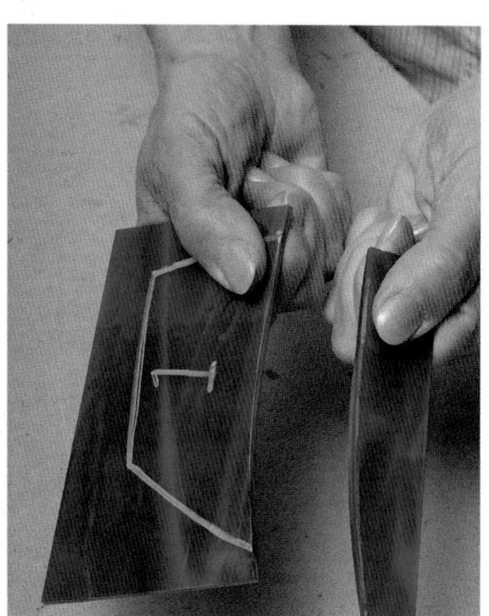

PRO TIP ✔

As you practice and become comfortable with all three breaking methods, you will discover when to use each technique.

Now score and break the remaining three sides, one at a time. Score down through the middle of the marker line so that you can see how you are doing. The scrap you break off and the finished pattern piece should each have equal amounts of marker.

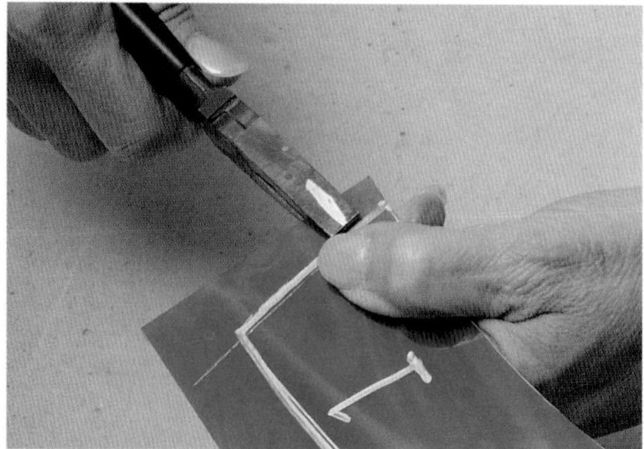

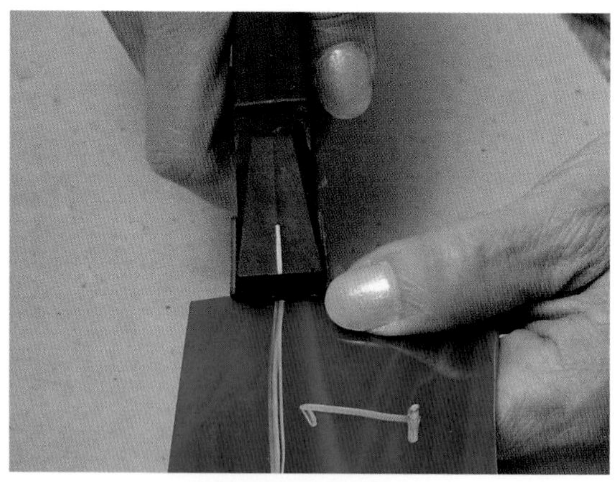

Cutting primer

2

4

6

5

1

3

Practice cutting designs showing cutting sequence

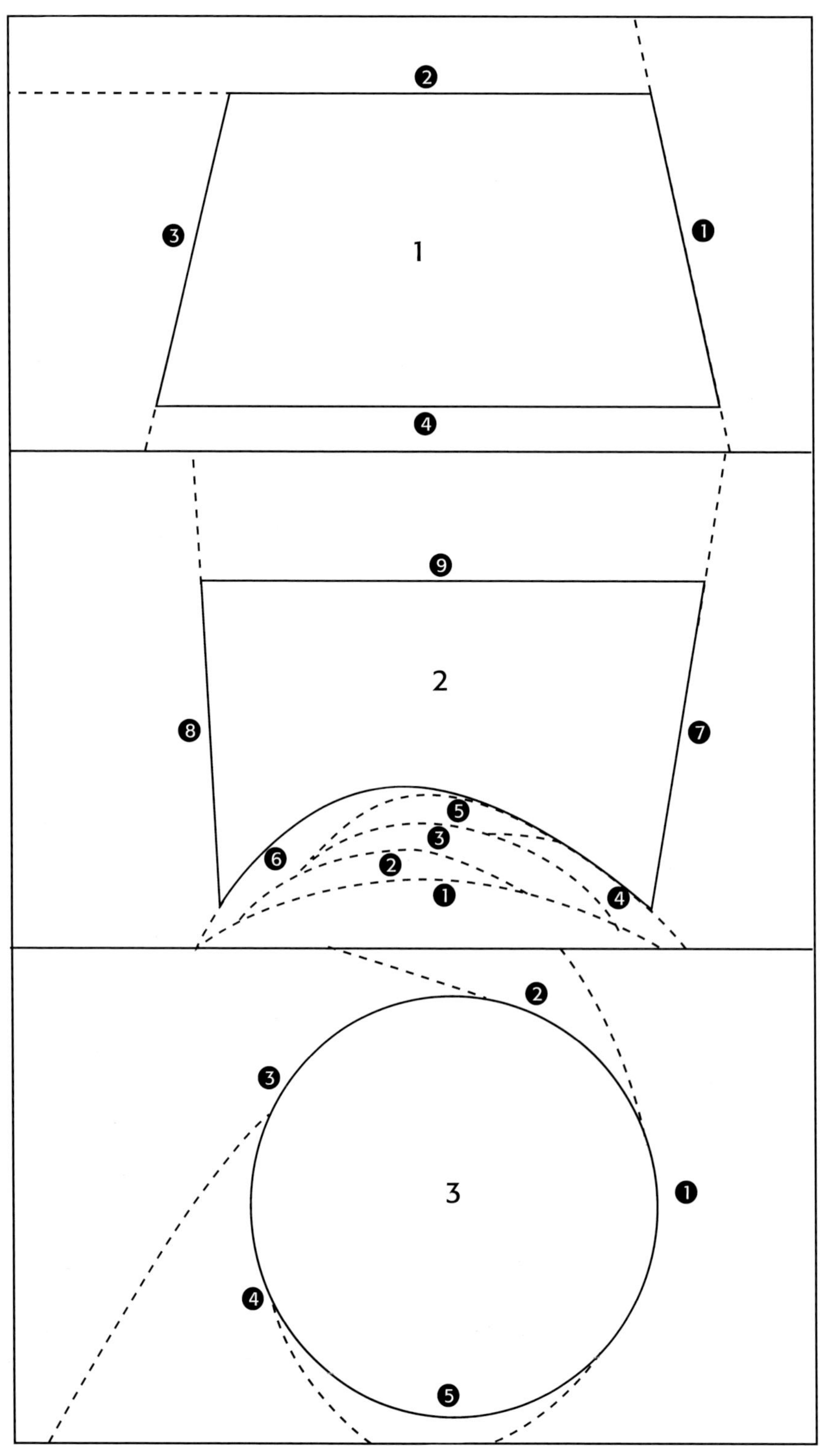

Cutting Inside Curves

1 Now draw Practice Piece 2 onto a scrap sheet of glass. This design represents the most difficult shape in glass cutting: the inside curve.

If you were to score the entire concave part of this piece and attempt to break it out, the glass would very likely crack across one of the lower points. To counteract this occurrence, the piece should be scored in segments (see page 24).

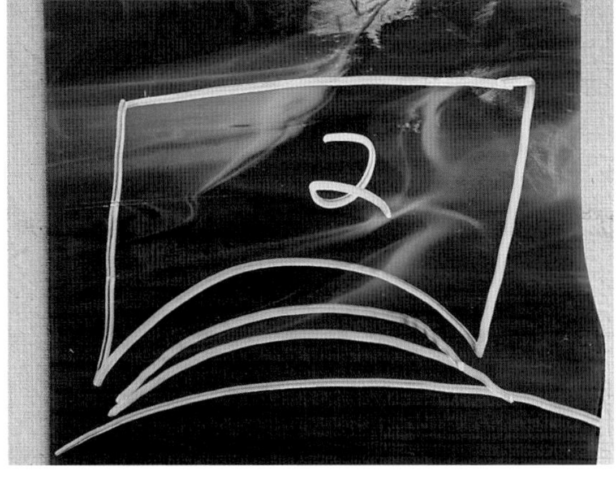

2 Start by scoring and removing the lowest segment with your breaking pliers.

3 Repeat this step for the next two arcs.

4 There should now be approximately 1/4 inch of excess glass left around the curve.

5 To further approach the original arc of the pattern, use a marker to segment the remaining area into a series of smaller arcs as shown.

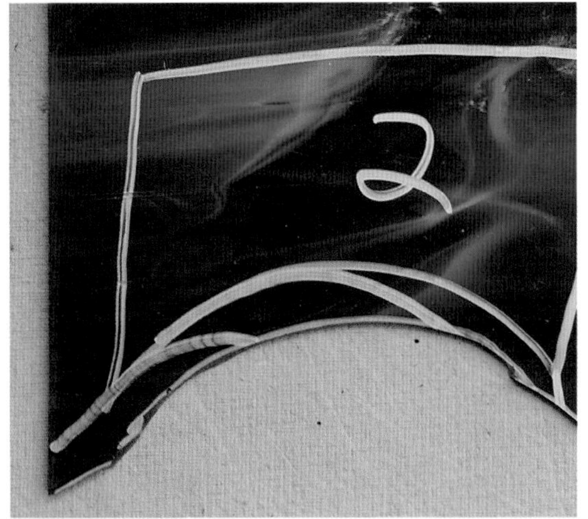

6 Start with the lower left arc and remove it.

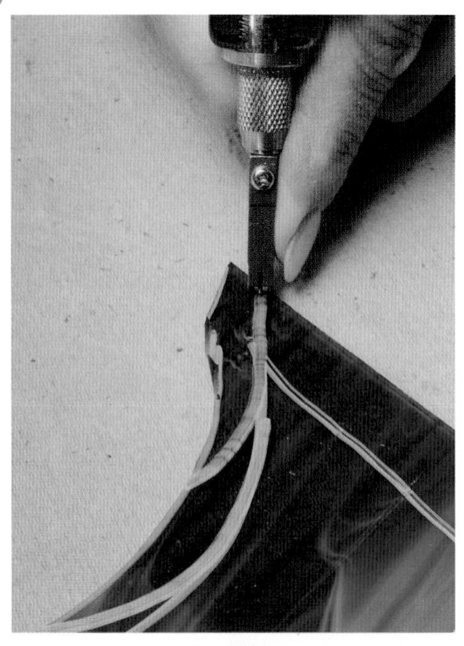

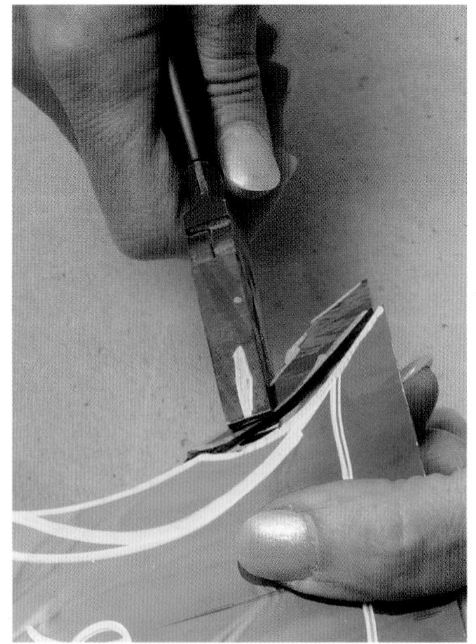

7 Continue to the middle arc, then move to the right arc.

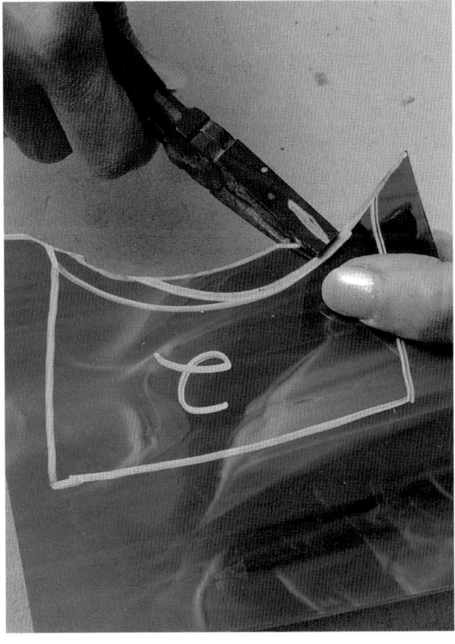

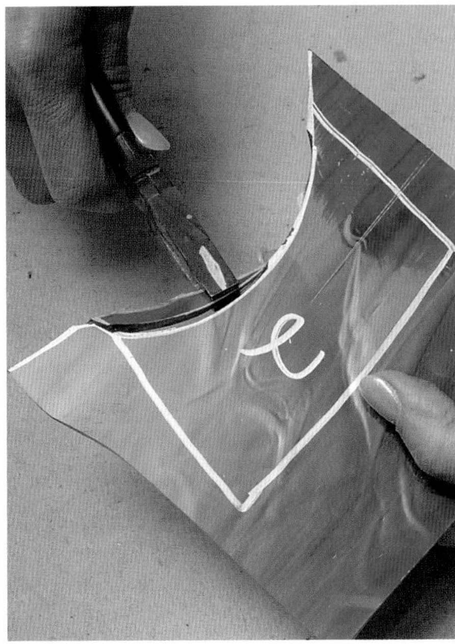

8 Complete the piece by removing the top section, followed by the two side pieces.

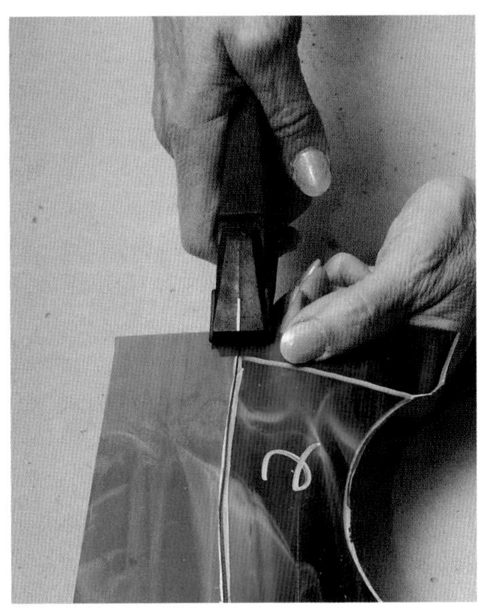

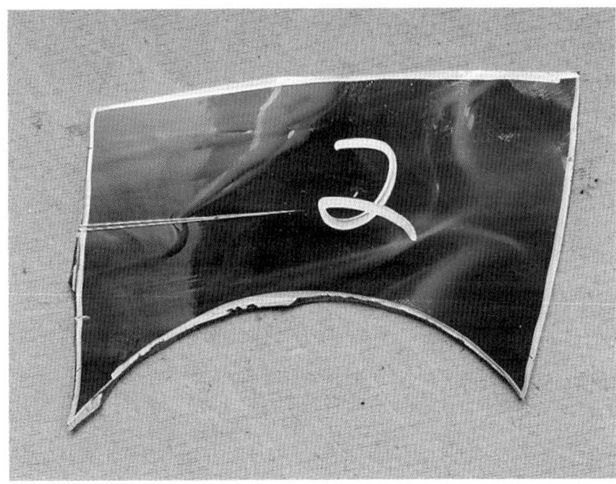

PRO TIP ✔

Avoid setting down your pliers on the actual pattern piece—they can scratch or chip your glass.

Cutting Circles

Circles are simply a series of outside curves. They should also be cut in segments.

1 Draw Pattern Piece 3 (see page 23) on a piece of glass, then add the dotted lines as illustrated.

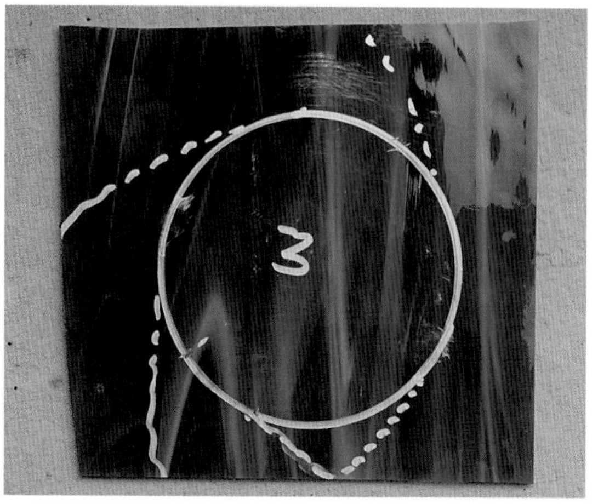

2 Your first score and break will be on the arc that starts at the bottom center of the piece and proceeds up the right side.

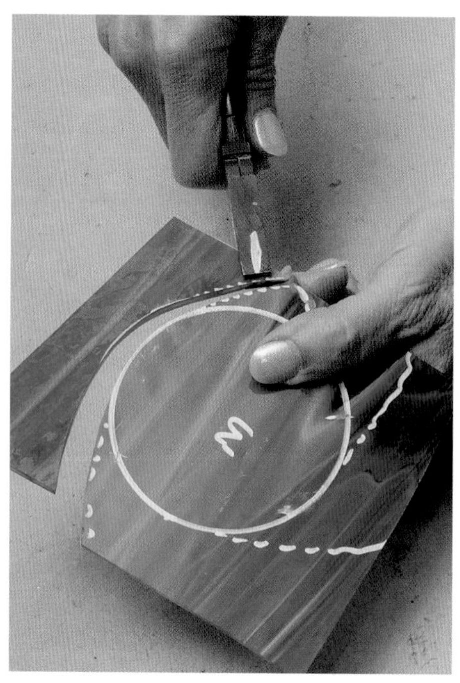

3 Continue with the remaining arcs right to left.

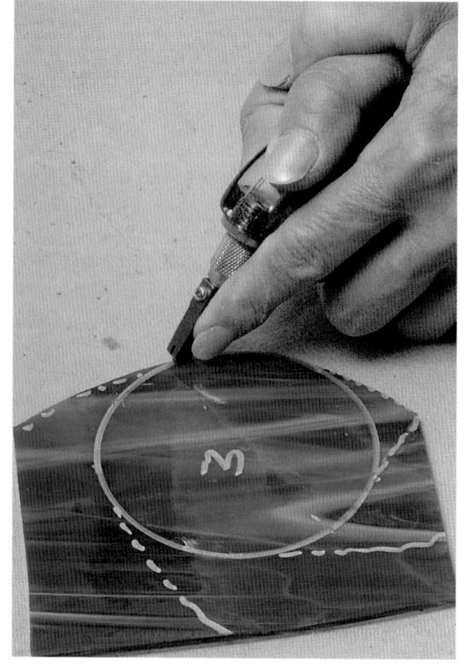

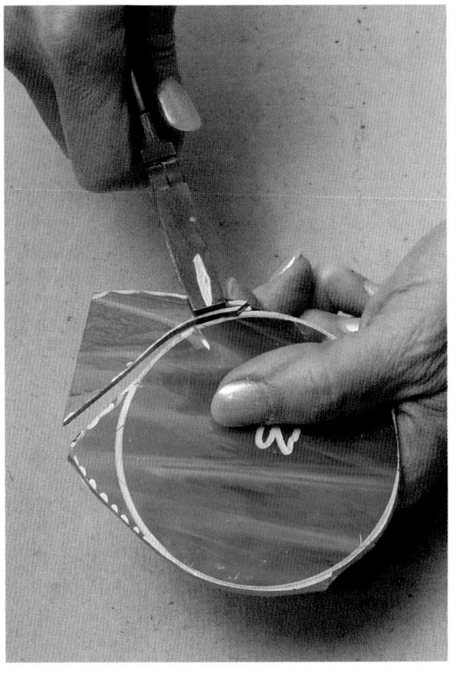

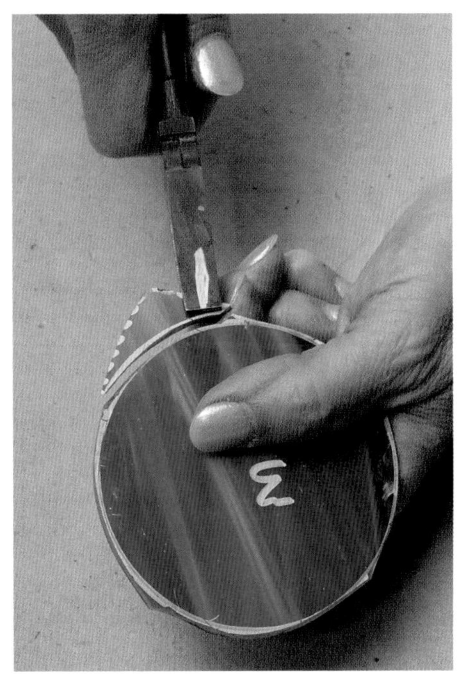

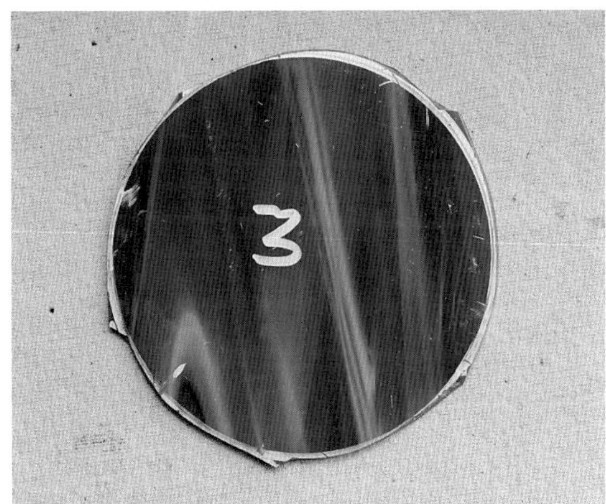

After cutting off the pieces around the circle, it's ready for grozing and grinding.

Cutting Strips

1 Take a sheet of glass that measures approximately 10 inches by 10 inches. With a ruler, draw a series of parallel lines 1 inch apart.

2 Line up the cutting wheel in the middle of a line, place the ruler against it, and position the ruler the same distance away from the line along its entire length. Holding the ruler tightly, run your cutter down the length of the glass. Break the glass with running pliers.

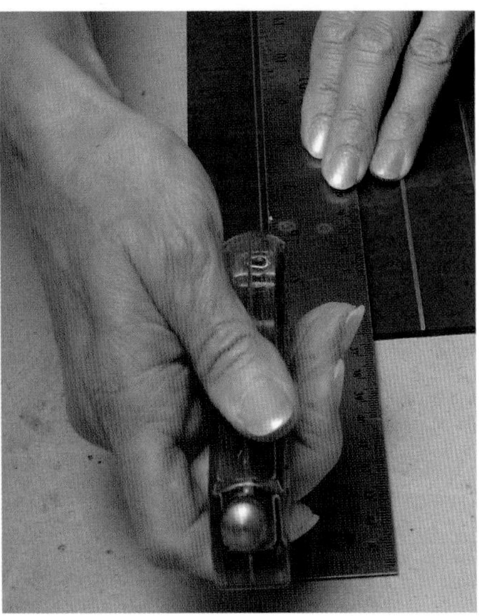

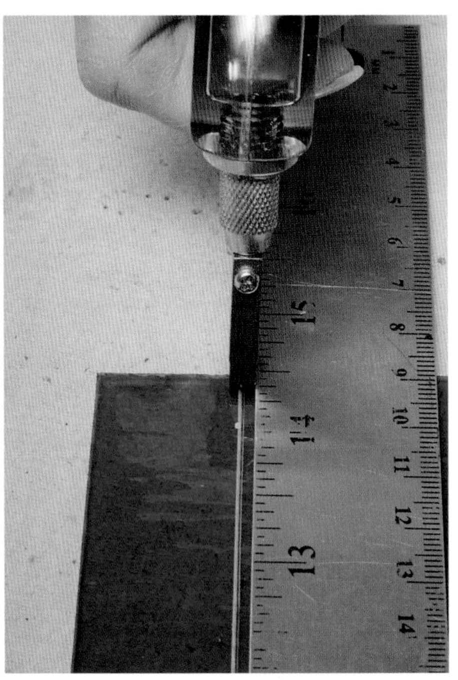

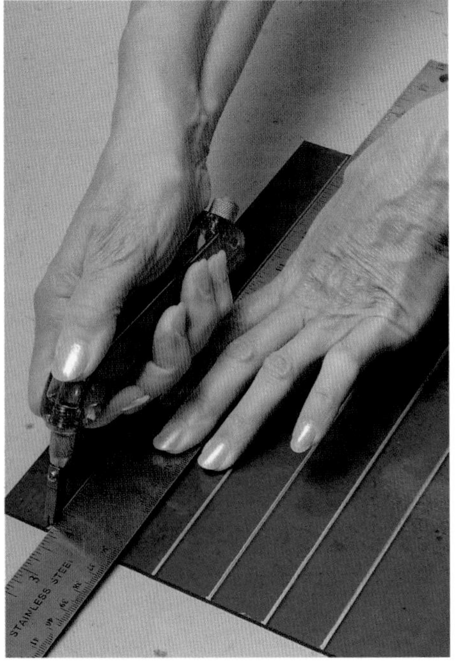

3 Repeat for all the other strips. Now line them up face to face and see how close they are in width.

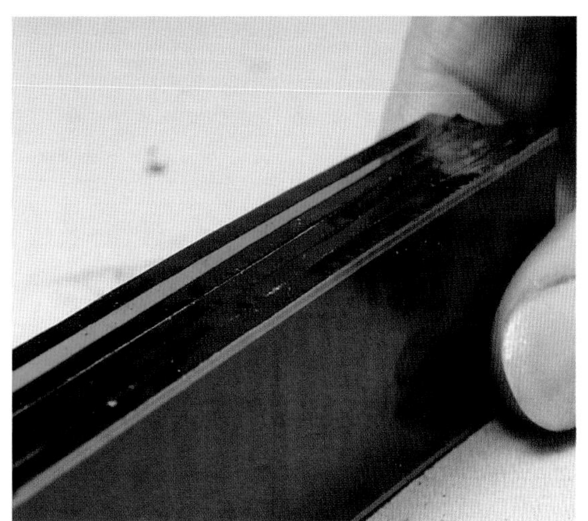

Grozing

Notice that on your practice shapes numerous jagged spurs of glass may still cover the edges of the pieces. These need to be removed by grozing with your breaking/grozing pliers.

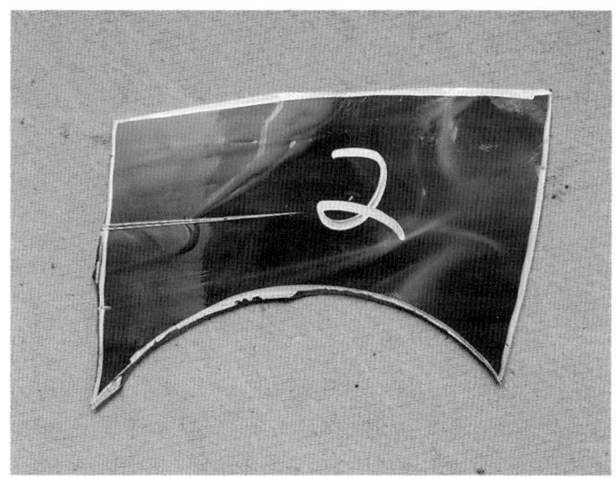

Grozing works best with the curved jaw of the pliers on the top.

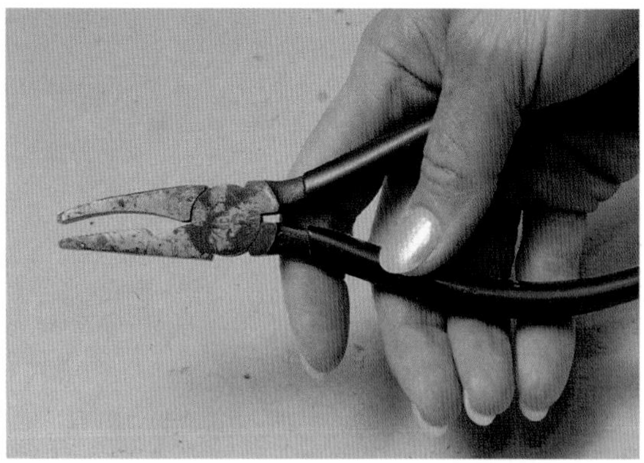

1 Turn the pliers so they are at about a 45-degree angle to the glass and put the jaws about 1/16 inch onto the glass where you intend to remove the excess.

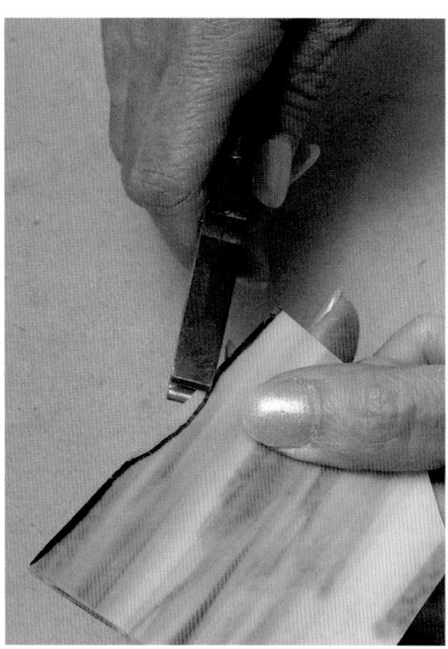

2 Apply a firm grip to the pliers and rotate them down and away from the glass. *Note: remove only about 1/16 inch of glass at a time.* Proceed along the area being removed, holding the pliers at the same 45-degree angle. You are not trying to crush through the glass; rather, you are pulling the small pieces away.

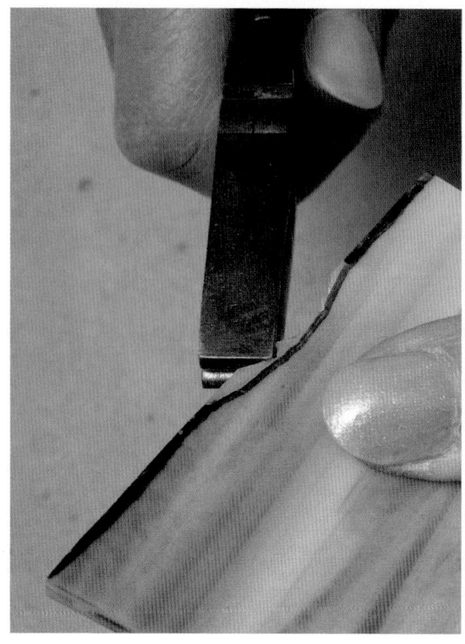

3 To take off the remaining rough edges, turn the pliers so that they are perpendicular to the glass. Place them on the glass no more than $^{1}/_{16}$ inch, hold them firmly, and rotate them down and away. You may repeat these steps in the same area to get your desired result.

4 Now groze the rough edges on the pattern pieces 1, 2, and 3.

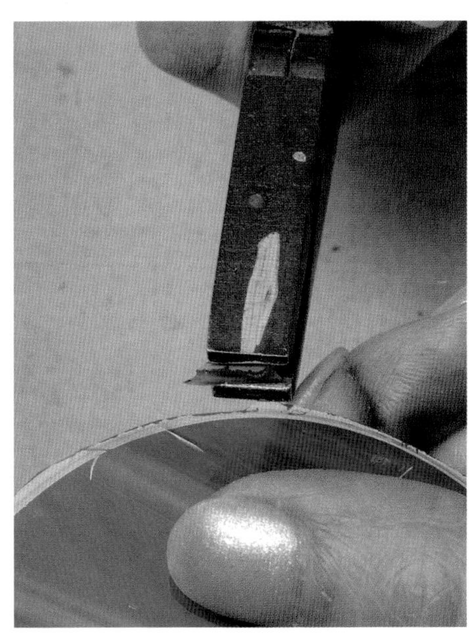

Smoothing/Grinding

The final shaping of the glass is done with either a carborundum stone or an electric glass grinder.

1 If you are using a stone, wet it with water for 10 seconds or so to keep the glass cool. Firmly move the stone back and forth along the edge of the glass. Never use the stone perpendicular to the glass; that angle will cause the glass to chip.

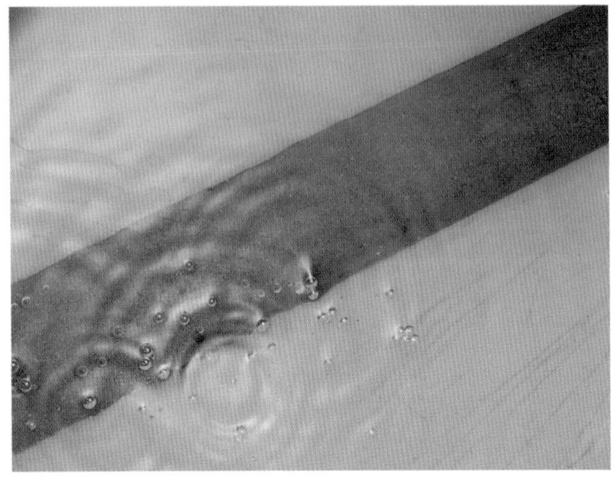

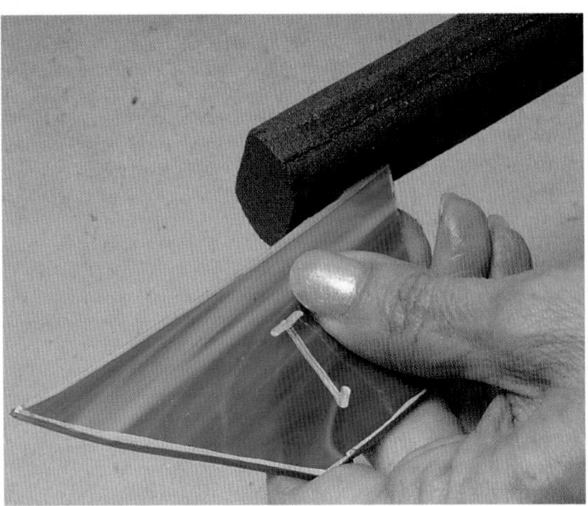

2 Alternately, you can rub the glass along a stationary stone to achieve the same result.

3 A more efficient method for smoothing lots of glass is to use an electric grinder. This specialty tool employs a water-cooled diamond grinding drum. Glass grinders are safe, fast, and very effective.

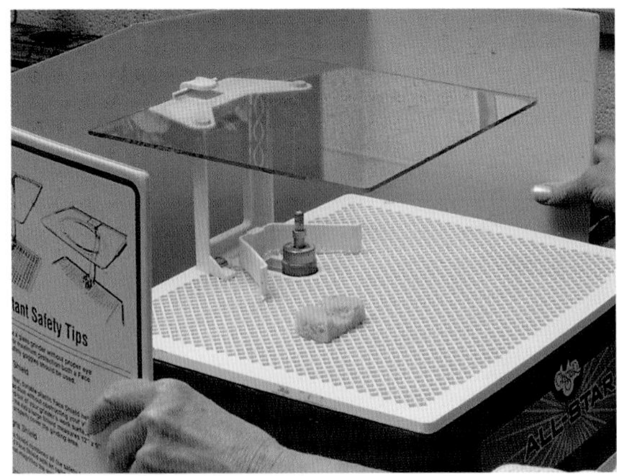

4 A small sponge is soaked in water then placed behind the grinder wheel, keeping the glass cool as grinding occurs. Lay the glass flat on the surface of the tool. Push the glass

against the wheel with a slight pressure, grinding right up to the pattern edge. A perfectly ground piece is one that shows no glass protruding beyond the paper pattern.

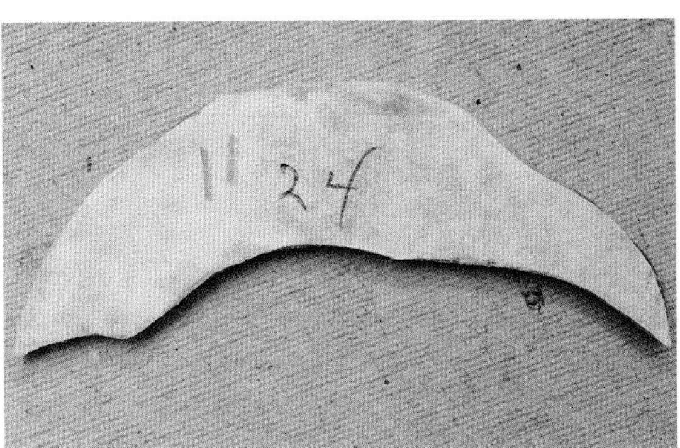

PRO TIP ✔

Push the glass in one direction and avoid a back-and-forth sanding motion when using a grinder. If you notice a buildup of dry powder when you are grinding, rinse your sponge and make sure it is making contact with the grinding bit.

More Practice

Cut the remaining practice shapes (4, 5, and 6) using scrap glass.

Then practice cutting out the shapes in the box design you have chosen. Shapes A–D are in the Victorian Splendor design; shapes E–H are in the Rose design. These shapes represent the most difficult pieces in the project. Practice cutting them until you have consistent success. Remember to use the principles you have just learned.

Now, if you have the inclination, try building the Exercise in Whimsy design on page 37. This design will provide good additional cutting experience as well as hands-on practice for foiling and soldering.

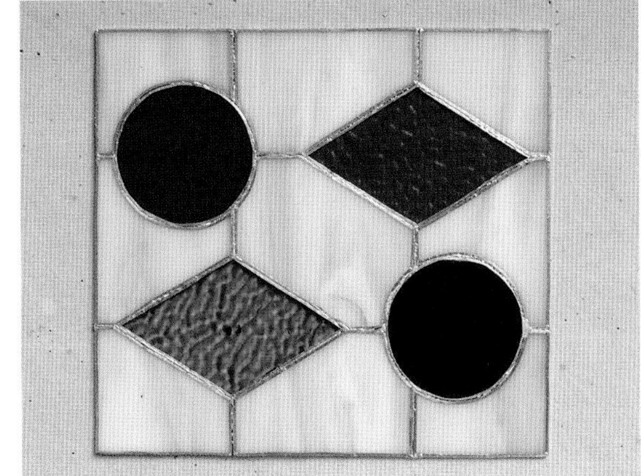

Practice shapes

Victorian Splendor design

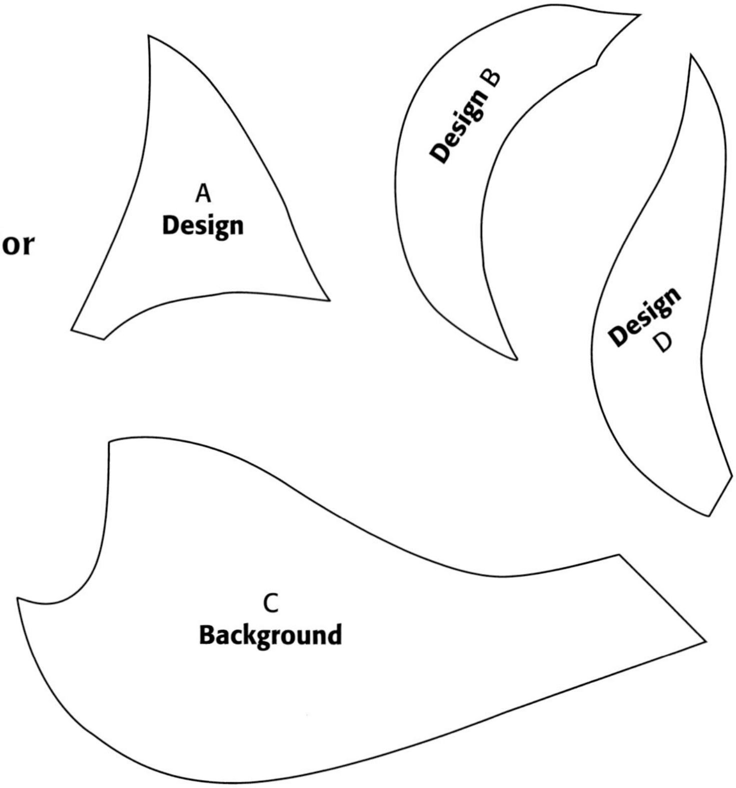

A
Design

Design B

Design D

C
Background

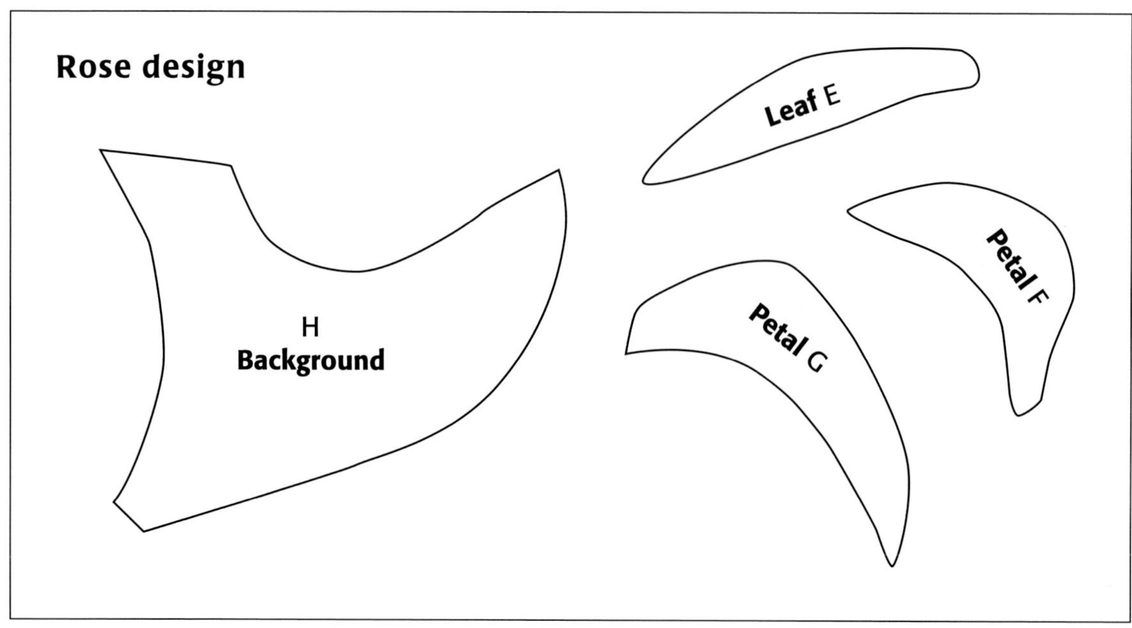

Exercise in Whimsy

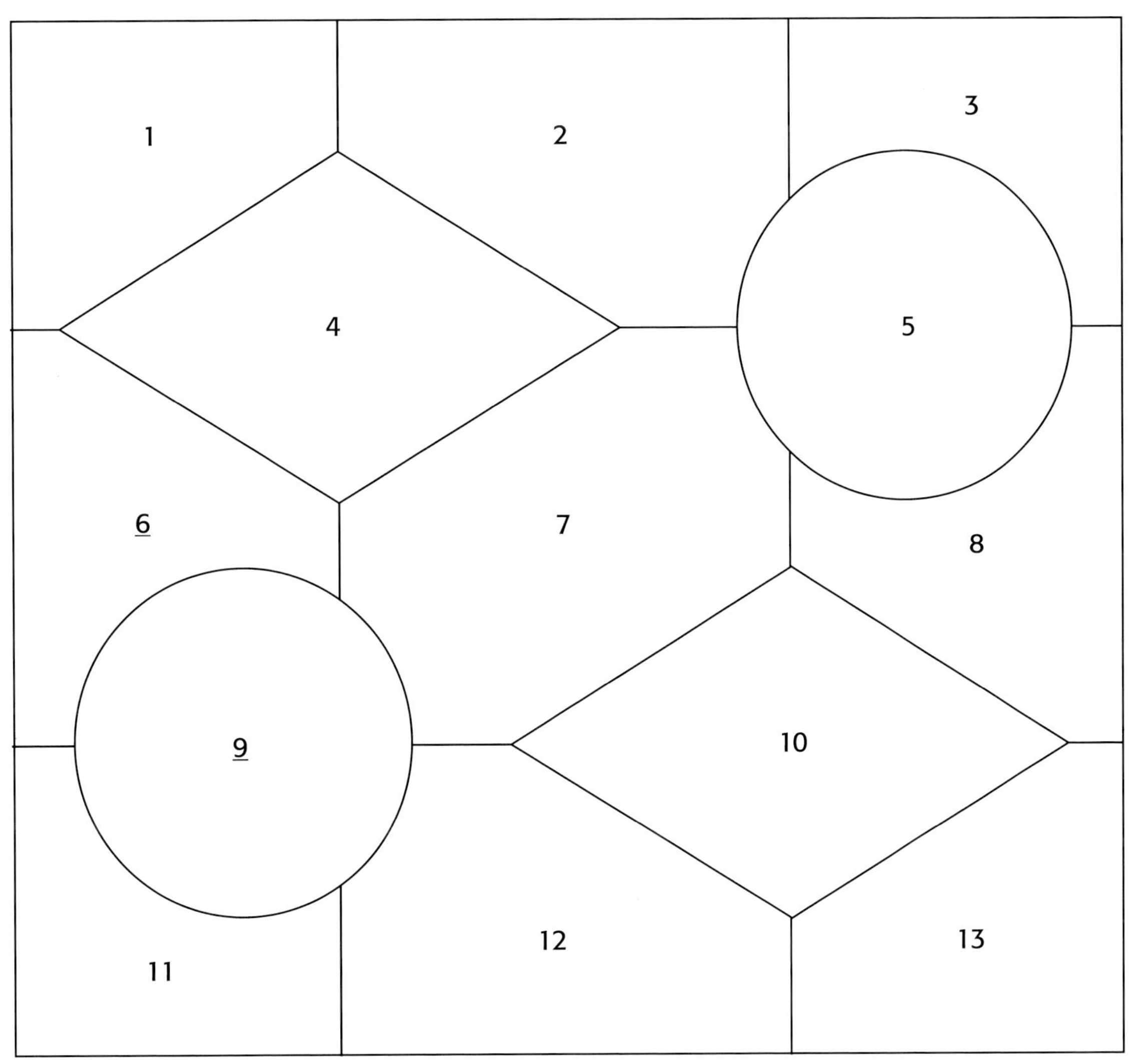

4 Soldering Primer

SOLDERING IS THE PROCESS BY WHICH A tin/lead alloy is melted onto the copper seams, connecting all glass pieces in a project. While providing strength to the project is an objective, aesthetics is an equally important consideration. The intent is to achieve a consistently smooth look that does not immediately distract the observer's eye. The glass should be the prime attraction, not the web of solder throughout the project.

Experience has shown us that most of our students tend to pick up glass cutting pretty quickly, while taking a bit longer to achieve acceptable results with soldering. The best learning approach is to acquire a few techniques and practice a lot.

In this soldering primer, you will be introduced to a host of techniques intended to help you achieve consistently smooth, slightly rounded solder seams. If you've chosen to build the "Exercise in Whimsy" panel, you will get an opportunity to hone your soldering skills prior to building your glass box.

Once you have cut and fitted your pieces, washed them thoroughly, and carefully applied the copper foil, it is time to solder the panel together.

1 Square the pieces on your work board with aluminum strips and pushpins.

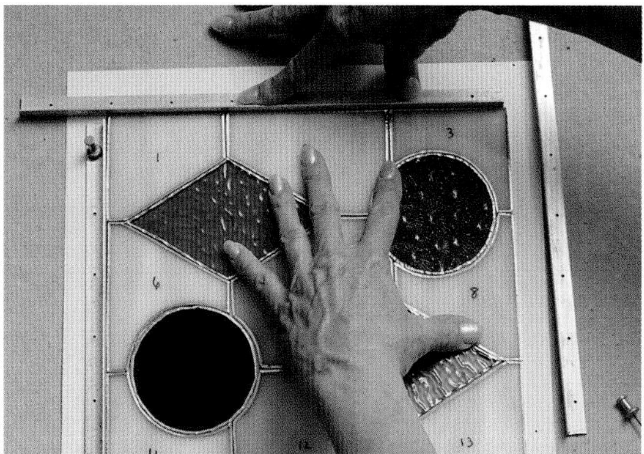

2 After you dip your brush in the flux, clean off the excess to avoid using too much.

3 Apply flux to all foil seams with a back-and-forth motion. About two brushes full will be sufficient to do one side of this panel.

PRO TIP ✔

For general-purpose soldering of most panels and boxes, 700 to 800 degrees F is an ideal setting for your iron. So how do you know when you are in that range? Touch the solder to the iron tip. If it melts instantly and stays on the iron without dripping off, the temperature is fine.

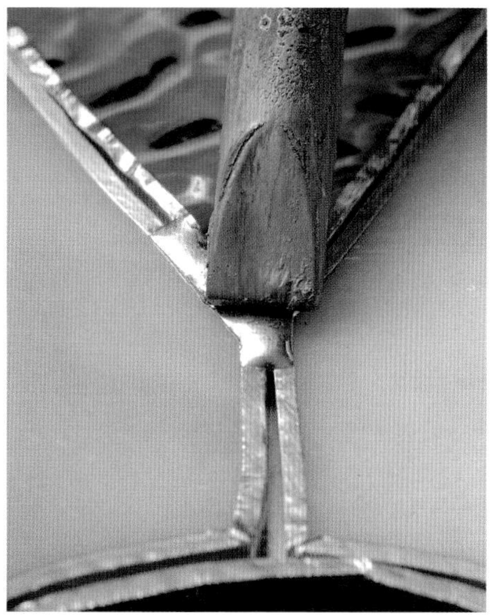

4 When your iron has reached a suitable temperature, you will begin tack soldering. This entails melting solder at all intersections where three or more pieces join. Unravel 6 to 8 inches of solder and put the end of the solder down at an intersection. Pinch off approximately $^{1}/_{8}$ inch of solder with your iron. Lift away the solder, and then lift the iron. Each tacking should take approximately 2 or 3 seconds. Leaving the iron on the glass for a prolonged period can result in cracked glass.

5 Finish all the remaining intersections. You will notice that ash forms on the iron as you solder. Get in the habit of wiping the iron tip on the wet sponge frequently to keep the iron clean. Wiping once on each side is usually sufficient.

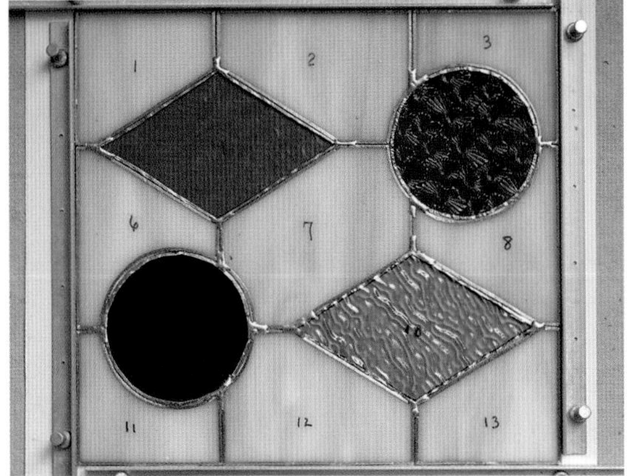

6 Remove the metal strips.

7 For the rest of the soldering session, hold the iron like you are shaking hands or holding a sword. The iron should be tilted at a 45-degree angle. It can rest on the copper seam. Touch the solder to the iron, and as the solder melts, pull the iron along the foil seam. Continue feeding solder to the iron as you move.

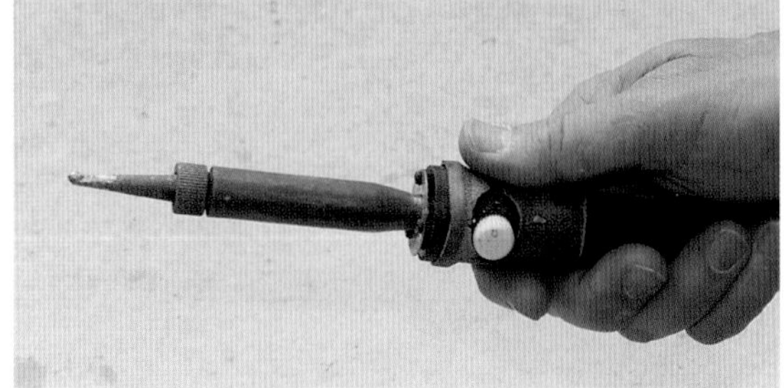

8 During this phase of soldering, your only objective is to cover all the copper with a flat coat of solder. You will dress it up later. First finish the front side.

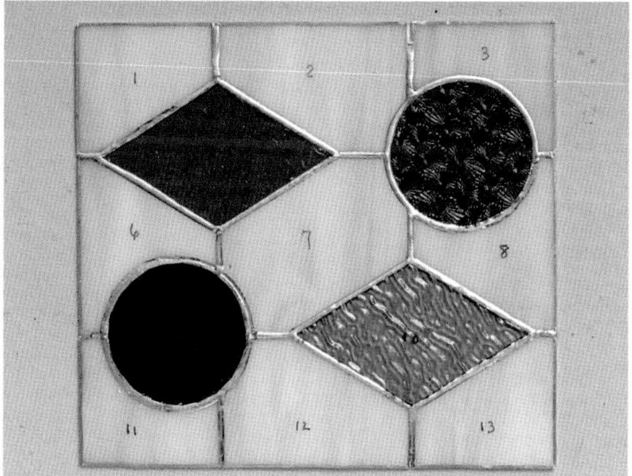

PRO TIP ✔

It is much easier to add solder than to remove excess solder. Use solder sparingly until you get the hang of it.

9 Before you start applying a final beaded coat of solder, brush a very light coating of flux on all solder seams.

10 The process for applying the bead coat is the same as before. Add new solder to flat areas and smooth out rough areas by remelting the original solder.

11 If solder builds up too much in an area, apply a little flux to it and drag the excess to another, flatter area.

12 Finish beading the first side. The look you are shooting for is a smooth, slightly rounded mound of solder throughout the project. It is important that all solder seams have a consistent height.

13 Turn the panel over and flux all seams. You will notice that all the gaps have been filled with solder, which means you will use a lot less solder on the back side. If you are becoming comfortable with soldering, try putting on the beaded coat during your first pass.

14 Frequently, flux will boil under the solder and cause a hole or pit to form. Simply add a small amount of solder to the area and hold your iron down for a second to allow the new solder to flow into the surrounding areas. Then lift your iron.

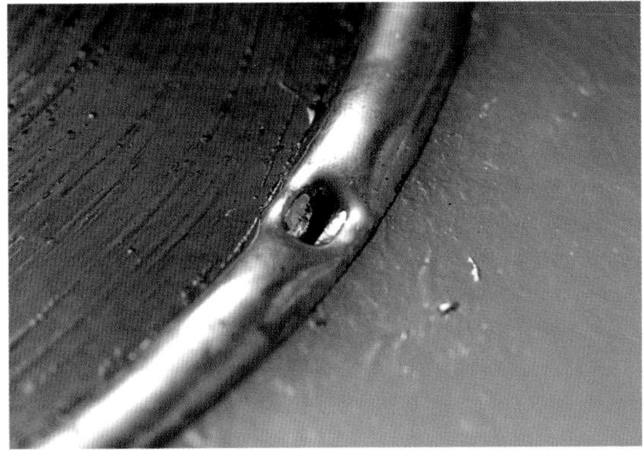

15 Now finish the second side.

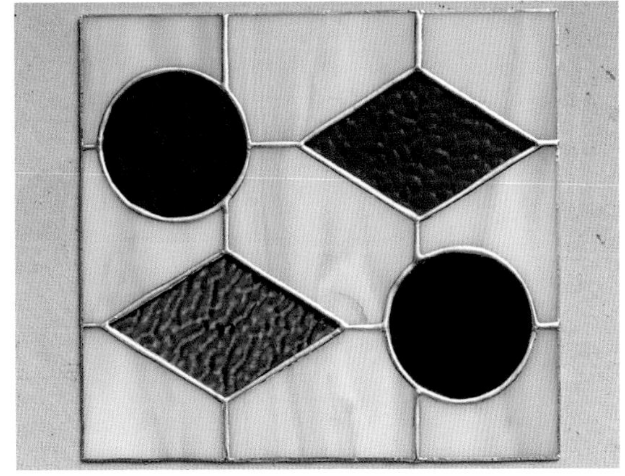

16 To finish the outside edges, start by securing the panel in notched holders as shown below. Apply flux, ensuring that it covers the foil not only on the top edge of each side, but also on the smaller overlapped edges. Melt $^{1}/_{8}$ inch or so of solder onto your iron tip and spread it on the foil.

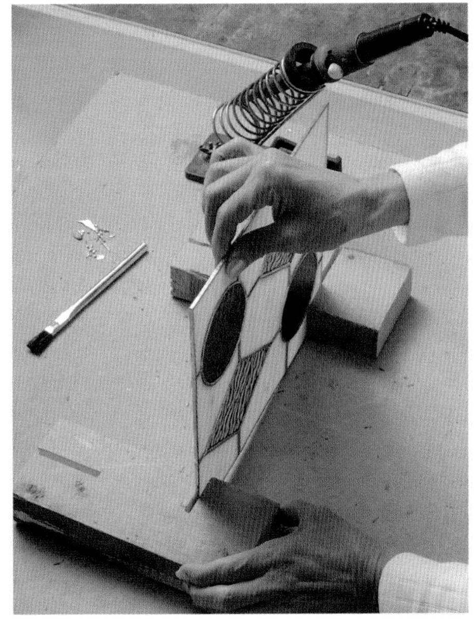

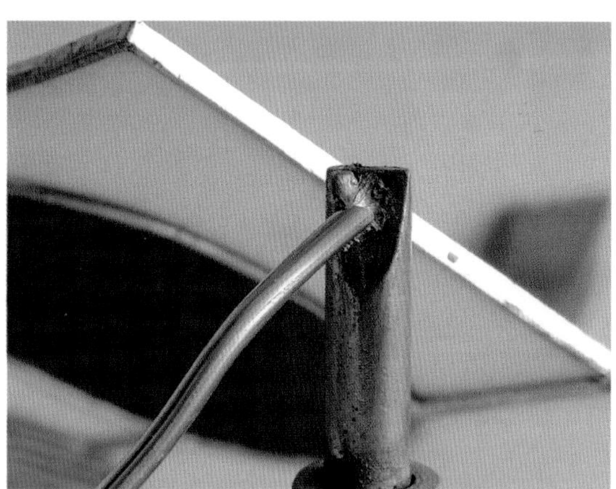

PRO TIP ✔

If the solder falls off your iron when you are coating the outside of your panel, the iron is too hot. Reduce the temperature setting or cool the tip with a wet sponge.

Repeat this procedure several times until each outside edge is covered. This process is called tinning.

17 Now lay the panel down and, with the same technique, cover the folded-over edges of foil. If an area does not seem to cover, apply light flux and resolder.

18 Now inspect the first side of the panel. Occasionally, solder will melt through while you work on the back side. If this happens, apply light flux and smooth it out.

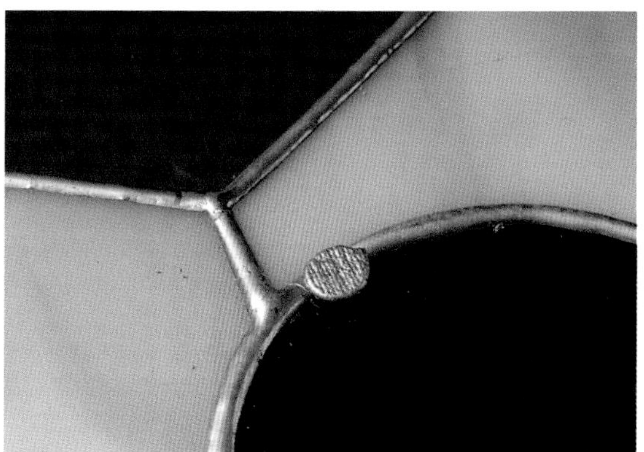

19 Soldering is arguably the most difficult of the basic skills to master. Be assured that you will get better and better the more you solder.

To further enhance your new panel, you might want to cut strips of a contrasting glass for a border or add bevels. Secure them with metal strips, and solder.

For details on framing this panel and attaching hooks, see *Basic Stained Glass Making* (Stackpole Books, 2003).

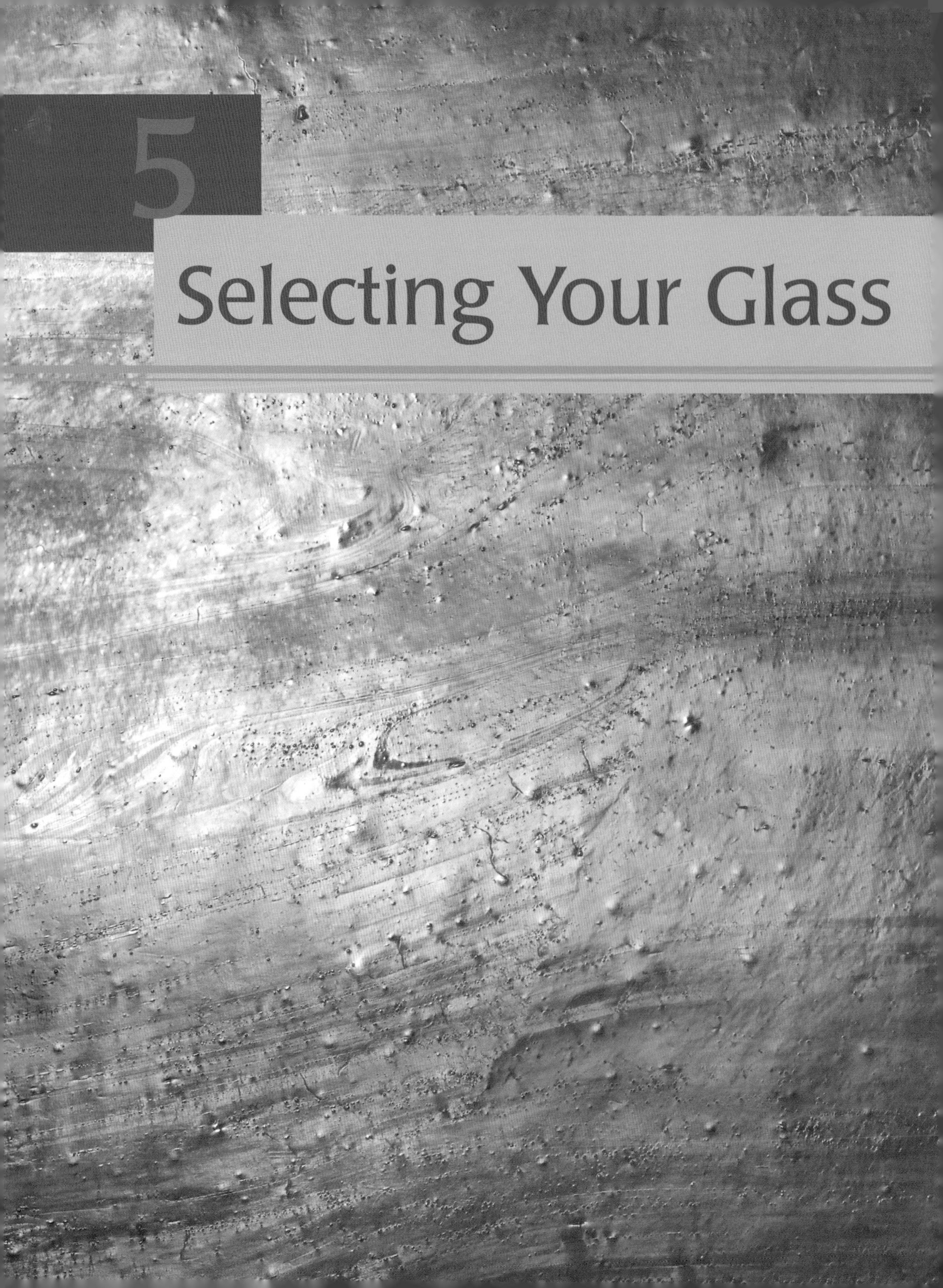

5 Selecting Your Glass

THE SINGLE MOST IMPORTANT STEP IN THE entire box construction process is the selection of specific glass types. Tightly fitting seams, smooth solder lines, and perfect hinging will all be overlooked if the glass you use does not work. This part of the process is also an opportunity for you, as the artist, to express yourself in this colorful art. Think of your glass collection as a color palette. Each time you procure new glass, your options increase. Soon, instead of thinking green, you'll be thinking about different shades of green or blends that might include blues, browns, and reds. Stained glass is a colorful art with many, many possibilities.

If you have limited experience in color coordination, a good learning exercise is to look through other stained glass design books and take notice as to what appeals to you and what does not. These authors are all professional designers and will provide you with various examples of glasses that go nicely together. Once you have studied others' works, you will be in a better position to express yourself with glass.

Because backlighting is not usually available to enhance the glass in a box, selection of glass should be based on the reflective qualities of the glass surface. This step is different from selecting glass for a lamp or window. With those projects, you want to consider how your glass will look backed by incandescent bulbs or natural sunlight.

The structural design of our featured box lends itself to glass that approaches opaqueness (glass you cannot see through). The bracing and support makeup of the box shelf would be seen if transparent glass were used on the sides and bottom of the box. All of our glass selections in the project examples are in the translucent to opaque range.

The next step in determining what glasses to use is to decide on colors. Make several photo copies of the design you are using, then use colored pencils to create several renditions. Lay them in front of you, study them closely, and even get another person's opinion. Then express yourself with the color scheme that speaks to you the loudest.

The following information about types of glass will further assist you when selecting the glass for your box.

About Stained Glass

Most stained glass can be separated into three main categories: cathedral, streaky, and opalescent.

Cathedral

Cathedral glasses are single colored and available in a host of textures, including water, seedy, hammered, granite, and glue chip.

Water Glass

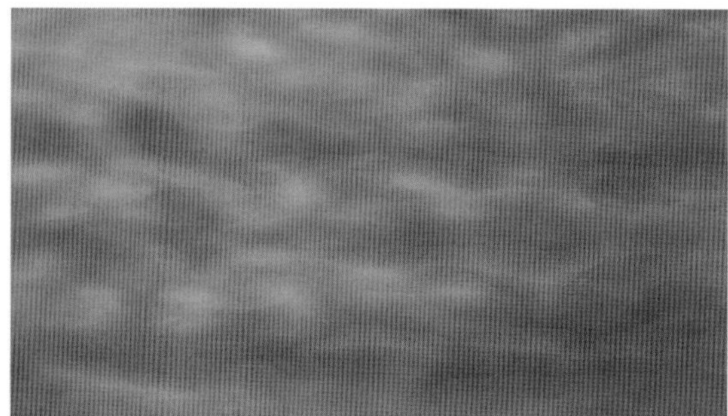

Glue Chip

Hammered

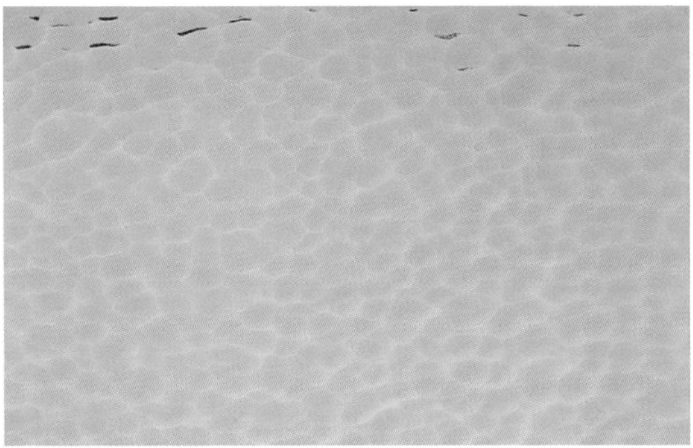

Granite

Cathedrals are transparent in nature; however, different textures will affect the degree of transparency. By using a seedy glass in a door sidelight, it is possible to maximize visibility through the panel. The same window when made of ripple glass offers a greater degree of privacy.

Seedy Glass—more transparency

Ripple Glass—less transparency

Streaky

Streaky glasses are cathedrals with streaks of one or more other colors of cathedral or opalescent. They may be smooth or come in textures such as ripple, water glass, or granite.

Opalescent

Opalescent glasses, also known as "opals," are made up of varying amounts of white (opal) glass mixed with colored glass. The higher the opal content, the denser the glass will be. Some opals are one solid color, but most are multicolored. The translucent nature of opals makes them the popular choice for lamp shades because the glass is enhanced when light from the bulb passes through it.

Wispy opals transmit the most light because almost three-quarters of the glass is cathedral.

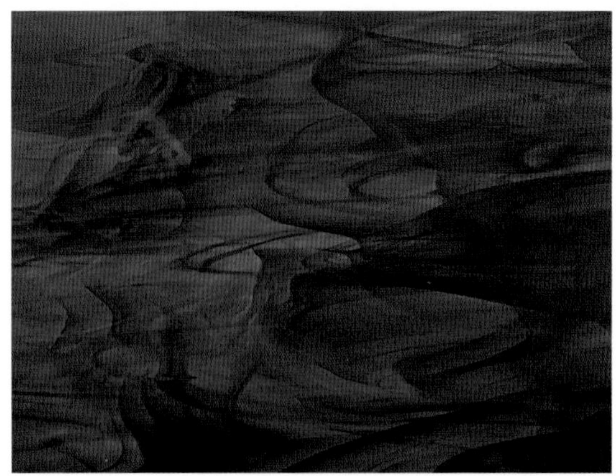

Translucent opals have almost equal amounts of cathedral and opal glass, reducing light transmission.

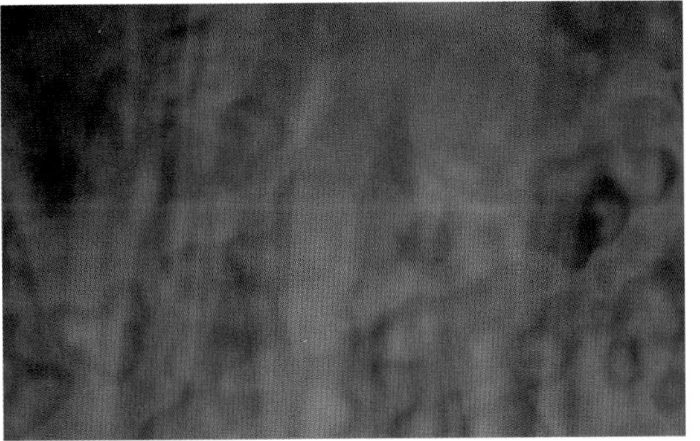

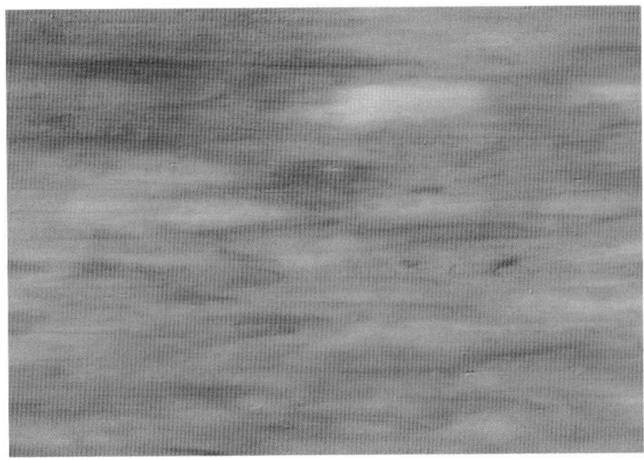

A new innovative surface available from Spectrum Glass is their Corsica texture. This resembles a soft granite finish and is found on the entire line of Spectrum's Pearl Opal glasses. When light is transmitted through this glass, the result is a very interesting sparkle (see Resources on page 153).

The pink/yellow/white outside border glass in the iris panel shown at top right is Spectrum Glass 606981 (pearl opal).

Semitranslucent opals are highly reflective due to their high opal content, and they transmit little light. Opal glasses are available in smooth as well as textured surfaces such as granite, ripple, or hammered.

Other Specialty Glasses

Other specialty glasses include ones with an iridized surface—a shiny, mother of pearl coating on one side of the glass.

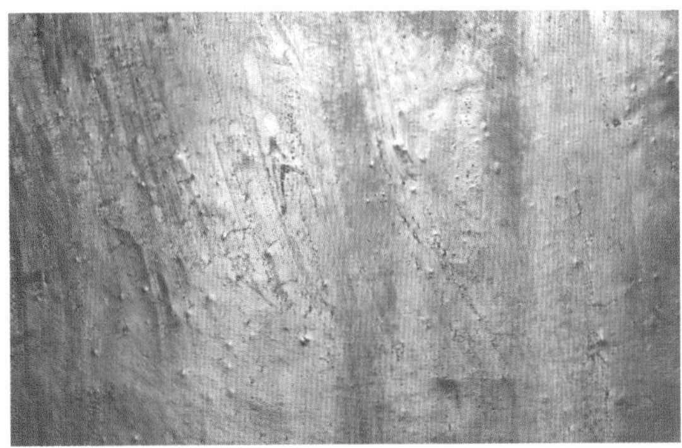

Glue chip resembles a frosted window.

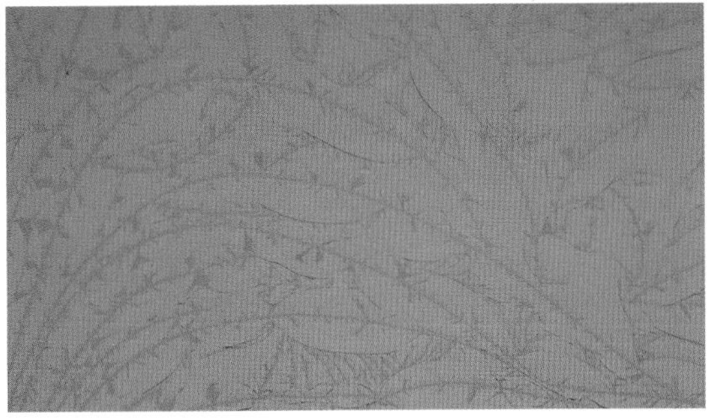

Art glass is usually hand rolled.

Uroboros multicolor

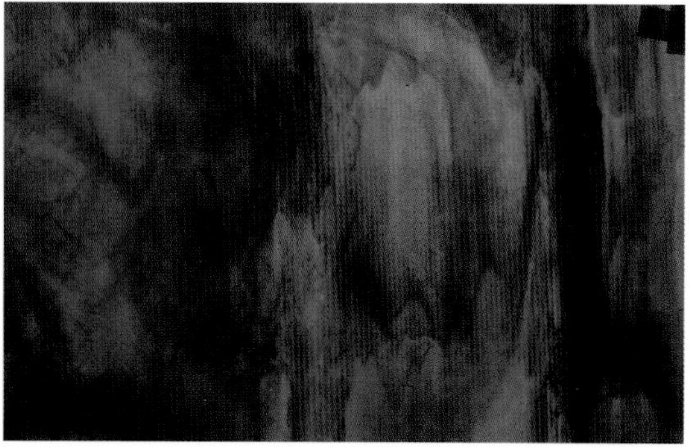

Youghiogheny stipple

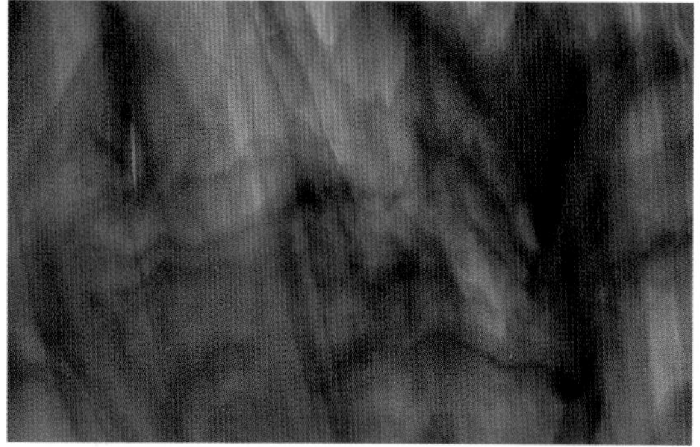

Van Gogh glass is painted on clear glue chip. This glass is totally opaque and has a wonderful almost three-dimensional reflective quality.

Bevels are precut pieces of glass with angled edges that create a prism or rainbow effect when sunlight passes through them. They are available in a multitude of different shapes.

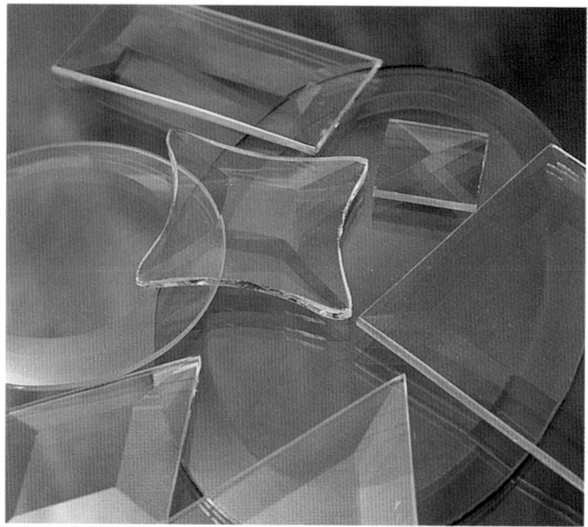

Jewels are faceted or smooth pieces of glass used as decorative features in stained glass projects. They are available in many colors. Three jewels are featured in our alternate box design Victorian Splendor (see page 55).

Rose

- Rose—Uroboros 6061 (orange, red white)
- Leaves—Uroboros 6074 (emerald, spring, light green)
- Border/sides—Wissmach 0218 (light violet opal)
- Background—Uroboros 0033 (honey amber mottle)

Victorian Splendor

- Scroll/ribbon—Kokomo 123 (2 blues); Wissmach 140 (rose/ white opal); Kokomo 654spl (teal/ white opal)
- Background—Spectrum 317.2 (medium amber opal); Spectrum 317.1 (light amber/white opal)
- Border/sides—Kokomo 86 (dark green/white opal)

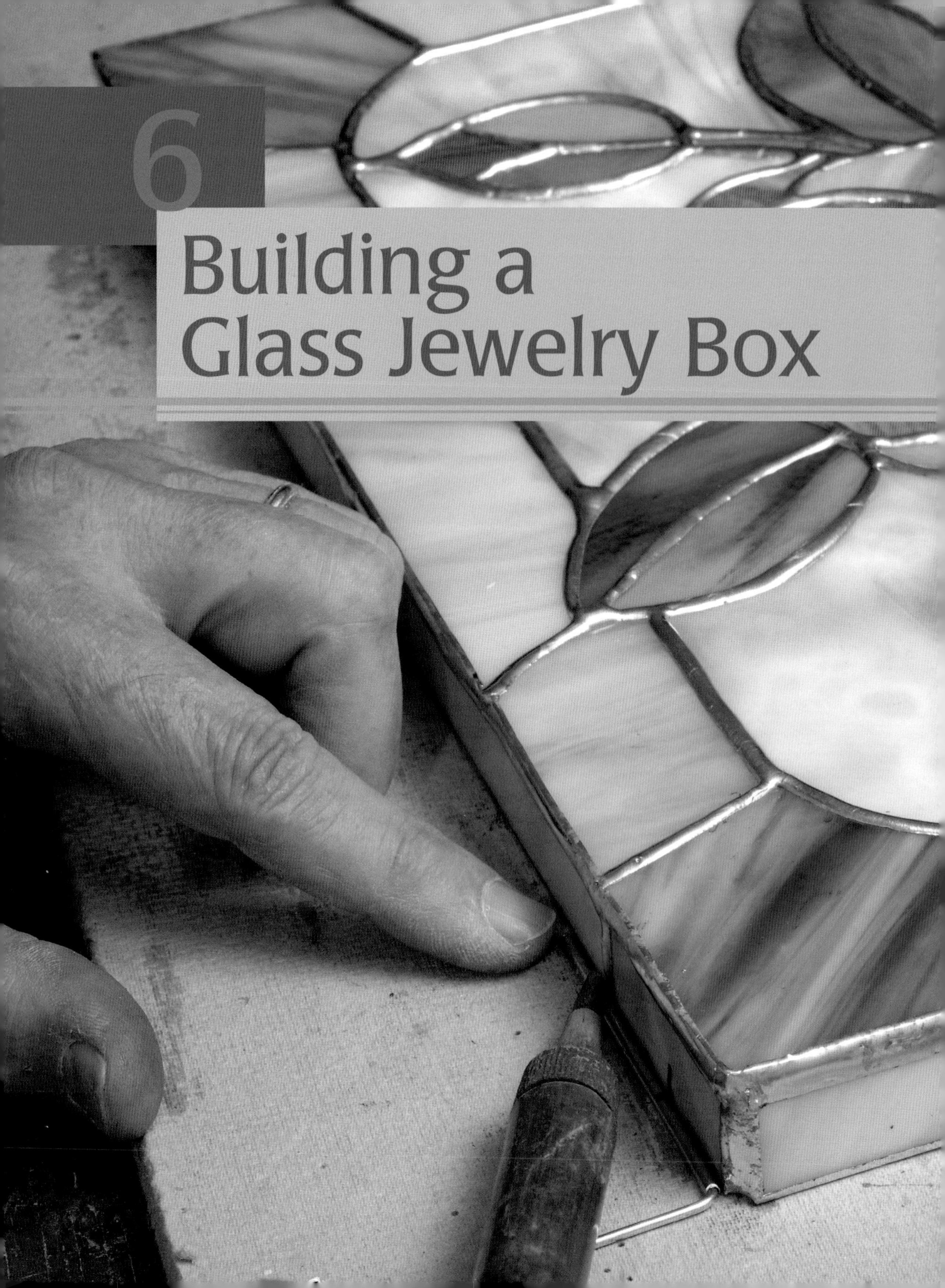

6

Building a Glass Jewelry Box

NOW THAT YOU HAVE PRACTICED GLASS cutting, copper foiling, and soldering, you should be well prepared to build your stained glass jewelry box. Again, you are encouraged to read all the directions carefully as your project takes shape. So choose either the Rose or Victorian Splendor design and prepare yourself for an exciting journey into the colorful world of stained glass box making.

Getting the Pattern Ready for the Lid

Enlarge the pattern you have chosen for the box lid as well as the patterns for the box components by the recommended percentage. Be sure the lid pattern measures 11 inches by 14 inches. (Pattern designs are shown on pages 128–131.)

Next you will need three additional sheets of paper, 12 inches by 15 inches or larger, to prepare the working pattern for the box lid:

- 1 sheet of oak tag
- 1 sheet of carbon paper to transfer the copied pattern onto the heavy stock paper
- 1 sheet of tracing paper to use for the templates to cut your glass pieces

Arrange the four sheets in the proper order starting at the bottom:

- oak tag
- carbon paper
- copied box lid pattern
- tracing paper

1 Place your pack of paper on a Homasote board or other hard surface. Fix it in place with pushpins or masking tape.

2 Using a ballpoint pen and ruler, trace all the straight lines of the design. You must press down firmly to ensure that the image is transferred from the carbon paper to the heavy stock paper. Lift up one tack and sneak a peek to be sure you are pressing hard enough.

3 Continue tracing the remainder of the pattern, taking care to be as accurate as possible. Go slowly, and stay on the lines.

4 Once the tracing is complete, number the pattern pieces in sequence. Numbering them will help you to keep track of where the pieces go once the glass is cut. Use any numbering system that works for you.

We started numbering pieces at the top left and proceeded to the right, then back to the left, and so forth.

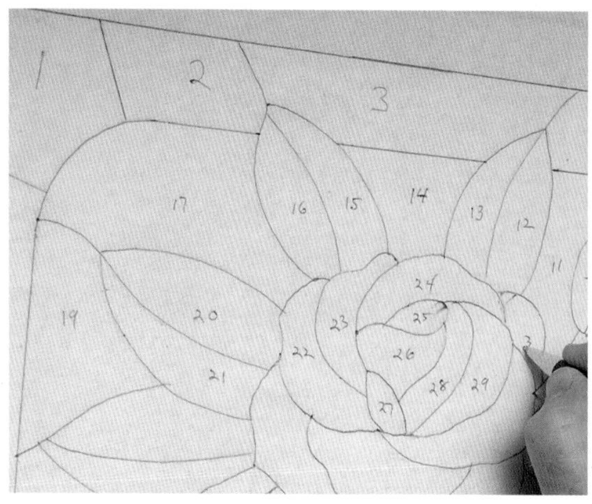

5 If you are using the Rose pattern, you should end up with 62 pieces for the lid.

6 With colored pencils, put a color stroke on each piece of the design to indicate the color of the glass you will be using and the direction of the color graining in the glass.

This step is important and will help you to build realism into your project as well as consistency into the background and border.

Typically, real flower petals have graining that runs from the center of the petal to the outer edges. Leaves have a grain that runs from the center vein out at an angle. By selecting glass areas that approximate that look, you will be able to create a more realistic rendition of the design.

Also, by running all of your background glass in the same direction, as well as the border pieces, you can create order and balance in the project. This unified graining will make the rose and leaves stand out more.

8 Remove the tacks holding the pattern pack and, using a pair of household scissors, cut away the excess paper from around the design on the white paper copy. Go slowly, and cut straight.

9 Now use a pair of pattern shears to cut out the rest of the pattern. If pattern shears are not used to allow for the addition of the copper foil, the project will grow in size by as much as 1/4 inch and will not line up properly on the box sides.

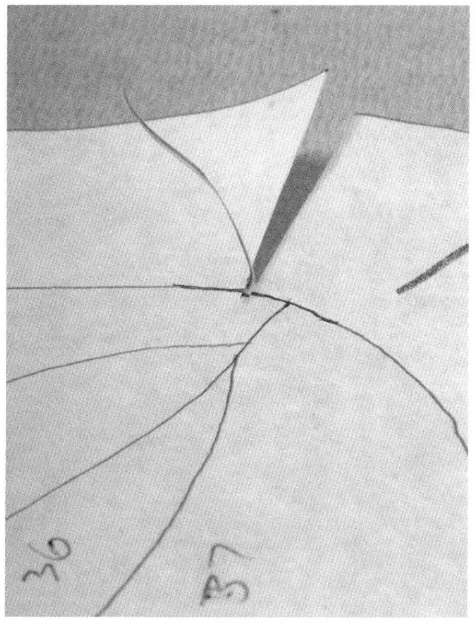

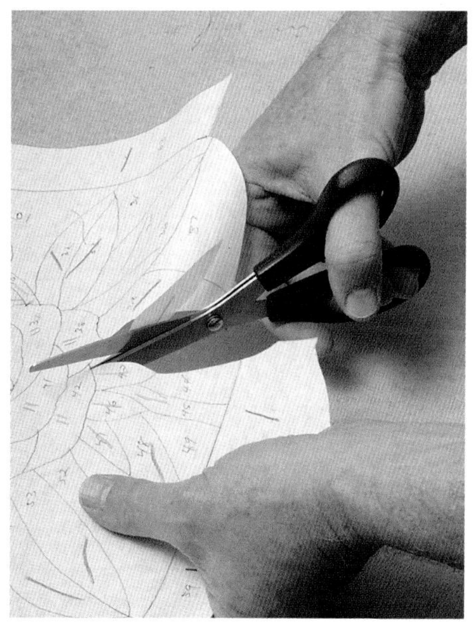

10 When the pattern is cut apart, separate the pieces by color.

PRO TIP: USING PATTERN SHEARS ✔

1 The single blade should be on top.

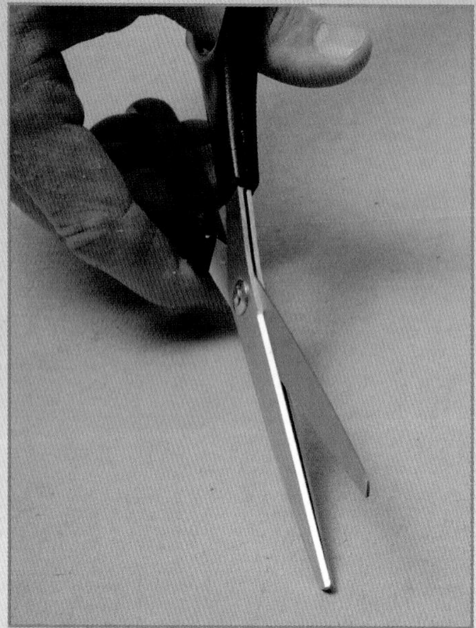

2 Open the shears wide and cut down no more than half way. At the halfway point, open the shears and move them forward before cutting again.

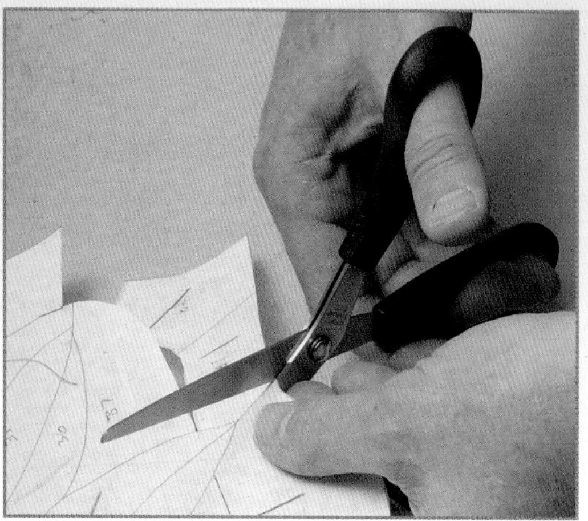

3 Avoid short, choppy cuts, as they will give you ragged edges.

4 If the shears get jammed with paper, quickly open and close them a couple of times to remove the excess.

5 Occasionally, because of the angle at which you are holding the pattern shears, the paper gets folded over rather than cut off evenly. If this happens, use regular scissors to cut off the area that folded over.

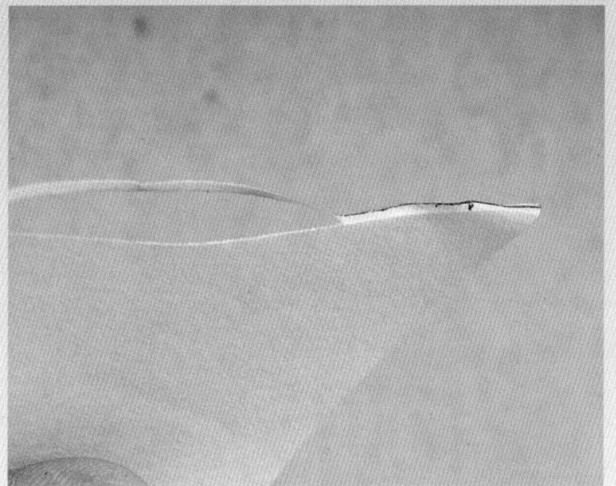

6 Never use pattern shears for cutting copper foil or wire as they will dull quickly and not cut your patterns cleanly.

Affixing Pieces to the Glass

With your palette of glass in front of you, begin laying the pattern pieces on the glass. The rule for glass cutting is that you should always cut on the smooth side of the glass. If both sides are rough, choose the smoother one; if you cannot tell, choose either one. With this rule in mind, apply rubber cement to the back of the pattern piece and adhere it to the smoother side of the glass. Make sure the color stroke is aligned with the proper grain flow. Now is the time to pick and choose specific areas of the glass you want to use to maximize the look of the project. Bear in mind that some areas of sheet glass are not as exciting as others.

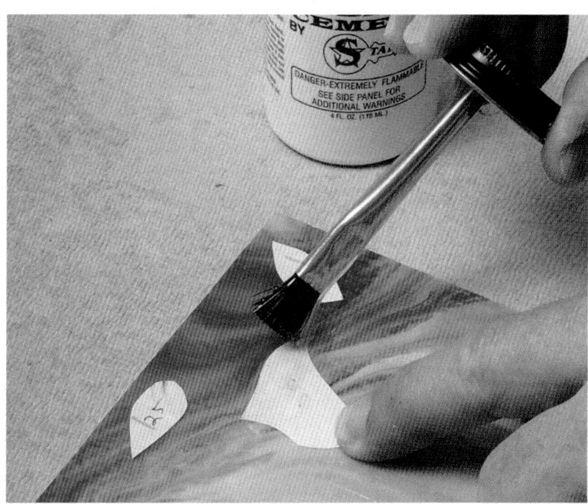

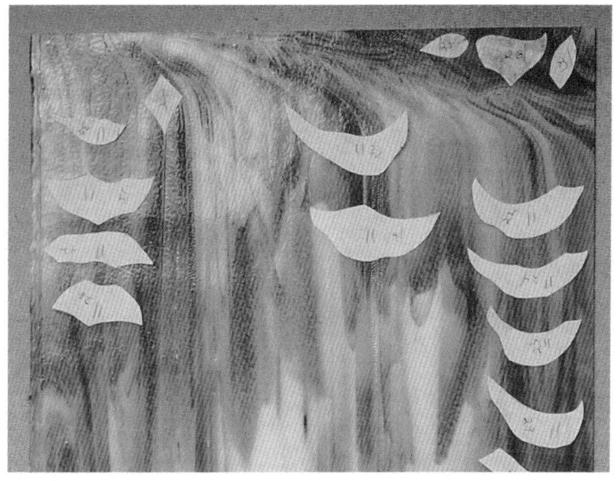

11 As you proceed with the rubber cement, be sure to place the pattern pieces so that they can be easily separated at the onset of cutting. As a rule of thumb, keep at least $^1/_2$ inch between pieces.

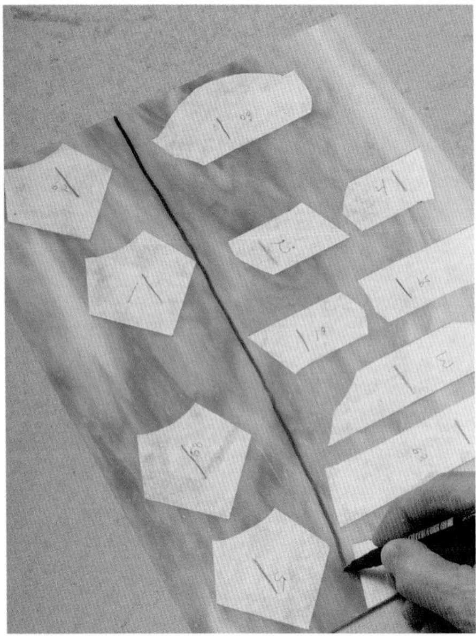

12 Putting pieces of similar sizes in rows or columns allows you to easily separate the pattern pieces.

Cutting the Glass

When all the pattern pieces are attached to the glass sheets, it is time to cut the glass pieces. It is important to cut the glass accurately so that the design will fit together within the 11-inch by 14-inch rectangle.

1 Begin cutting the rows of glass apart by applying pressure on your cutter. Proceed with a consistent speed to the opposite side of the glass. You should need about 5 or 6 seconds to cut a fairly straight 12-inch piece.

2 If you have not cut much glass or are working with glass that you are not sure how it breaks, start with some of the easier pieces. Typically these are the rectangles, slight curves, and so on. Once you are feeling comfortable with the cutting, finish cutting all the pieces. Remember that the nemesis of the glass cutter is the inside curve. Cut these out in small pieces with reduced arcs.

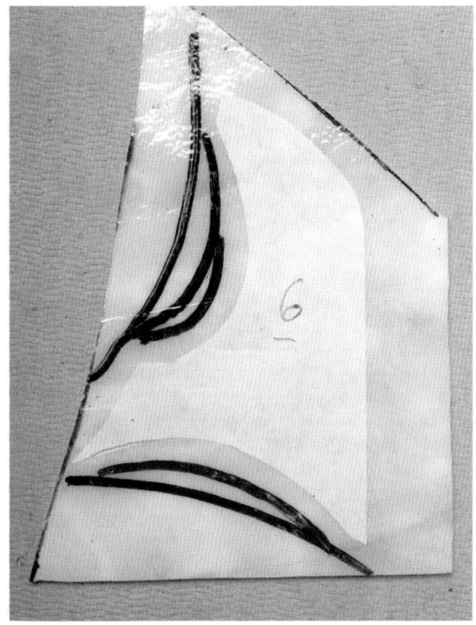

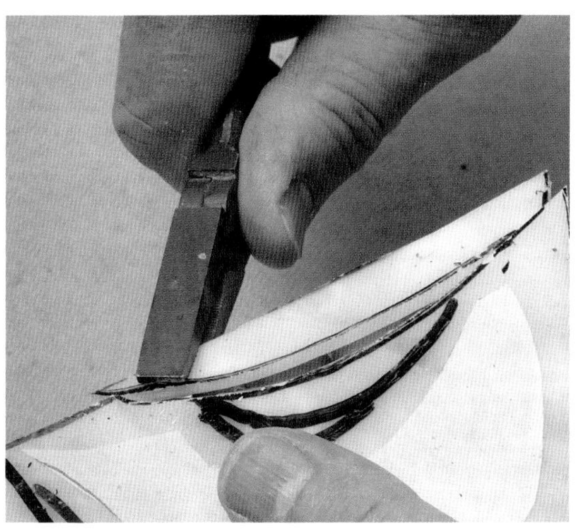

PRO TIP ✔

Important: Be sure to leave the pattern pieces on the glass through the grinding stage so you are able to determine where you need to grind.

3 In the event that you break a piece, simply peel off your pattern, apply new rubber cement, and adhere the pattern to a new piece of glass.

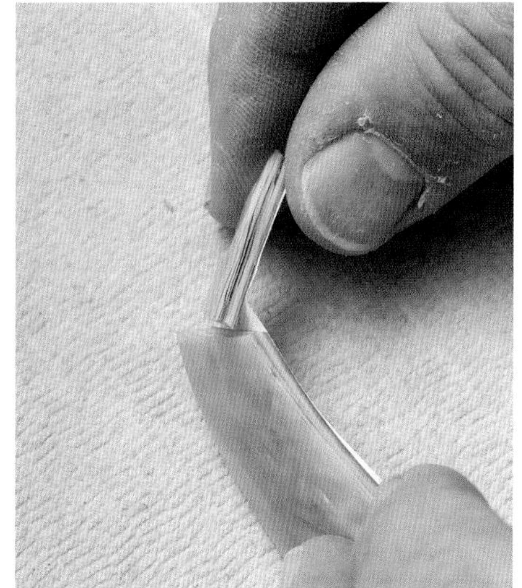

4 Cut all of the glass pieces for the box lid and place them on the heavy stock paper design. Do not be too concerned about the fit at this point.

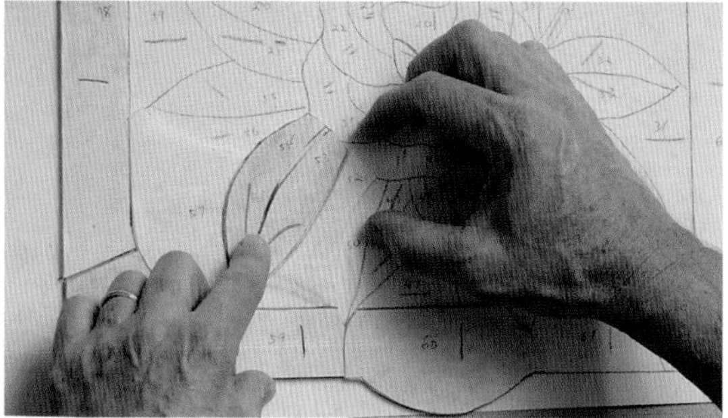

5 Grind each piece right up to the paper pattern edge. As you view each piece from directly over top, no glass should protrude past the pattern.

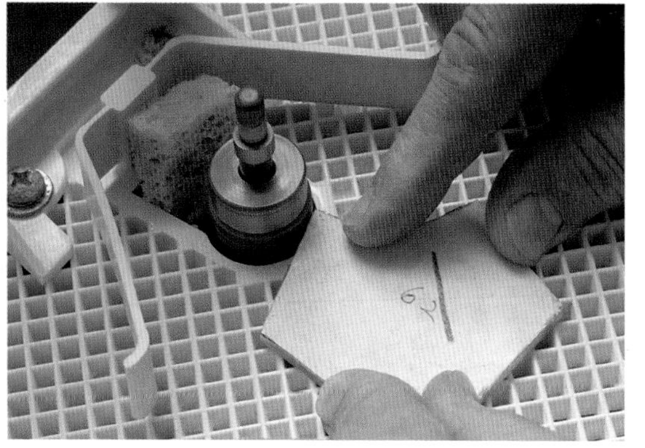

6 Dry the bottom of the glass, remove the paper pattern, and place the glass back on the drawing. Do all the pieces fit within the outside pattern lines?

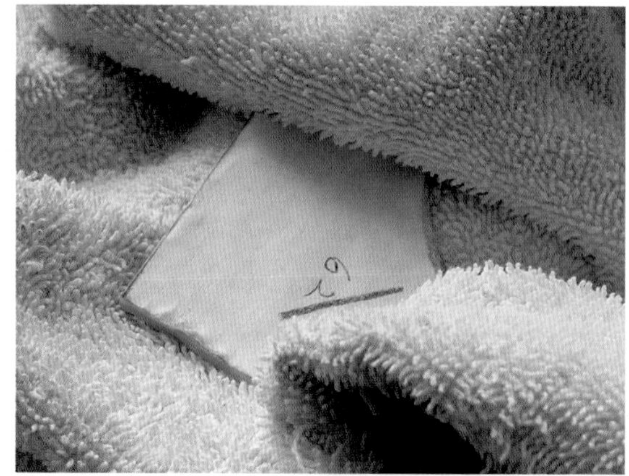

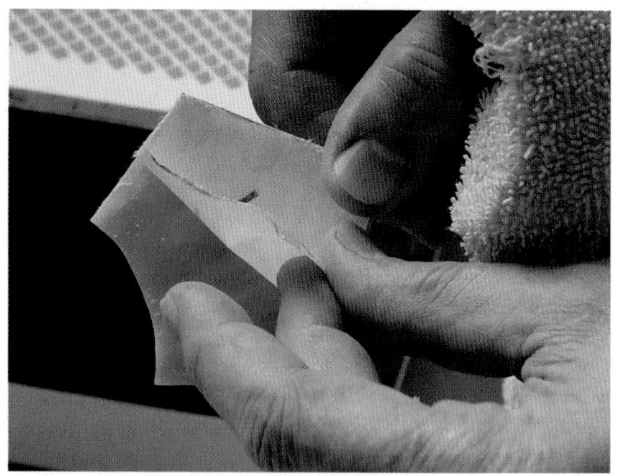

7 Now is your last chance to make any glass modifications. If you see pieces you want to change, trace them on a new piece of glass and cut on the inside of the line.

Grind if necessary and replace the glass. We chose to substitute a darker piece for one of the corners in our design.

8 With two layout strips, form a right angle with the left side and back of the pattern. The metal strips and pins should be directly on the perimeter lines of the pattern. The design should measure 14 inches by 11 inches. If any part of the design is outside the pattern lines, you will need to grind the pieces of glass that are causing the pattern to grow.

Washing the Glass

Before applying copper foil to the glass pieces, the glass must be clean in order for the foil to adhere properly.

1 Set up an assembly line with two basins (one with detergent to wash and one with hot water to rinse), the pattern board, a towel, and a foiler or a space to hand-foil.

2 Carefully slide the glass pieces out and away approximately 3 inches from the two layout strips. This distance will give you space to work as you wash and foil.

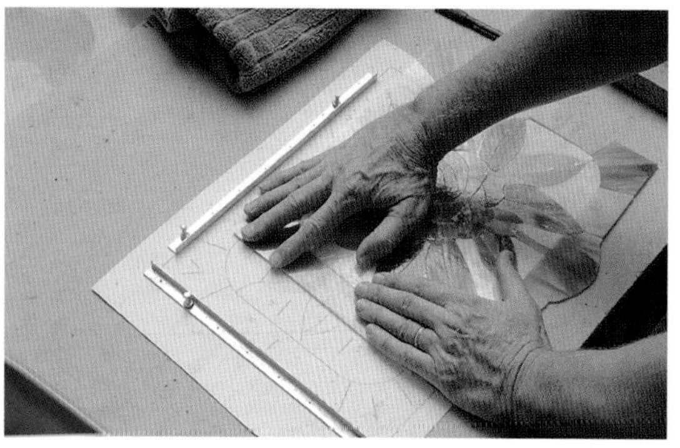

3 Starting with the top left piece, immerse it in the detergent and use the sponge to clean the outside edges as well as the top and bottom. Be sure to remove all the dust from grinding. Rinse the piece in hot water, then dry it with a towel. Do the same for all pieces.

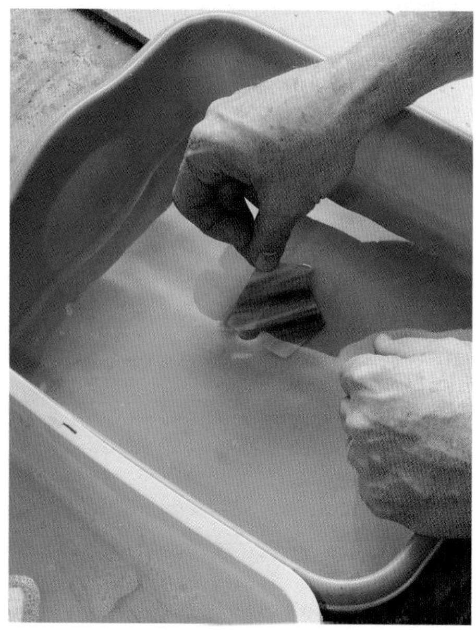

Foiling the Pieces

Because solder does not adhere to glass, each project piece must be wrapped in copper foil. Good foiling is very important, so try to be as precise as possible.

The recommended foil size for the box project is 7/32-inch foil, which is considered a medium width.

1 When foiling by hand, begin by peeling away several inches of foil backing. Allow the foil to fit between the first two fingers on your nondominant hand with the sticky side facing you. The waste paper will be behind your fingers. Center a small section of glass on the foil and press down.

2 Begin rolling the glass onto the foil, keeping the edge of the glass centered on the foil.

3 As you work, keep the strand of foil under light tension by pulling it gently as you press the glass onto the foil.

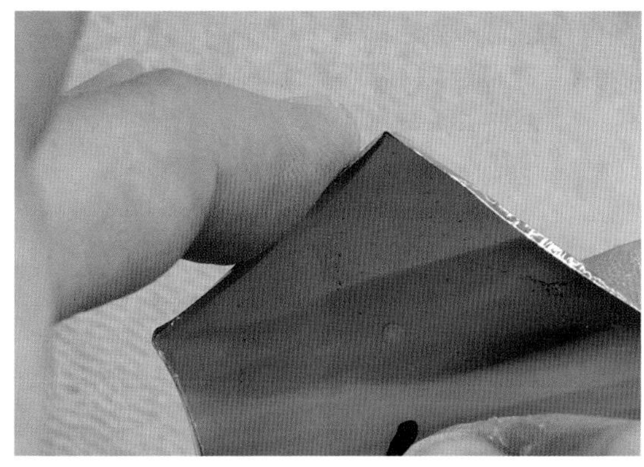

4 Continue rolling the glass onto the foil until you are back at the starting point. Overlap the ends about 1/8 inch.

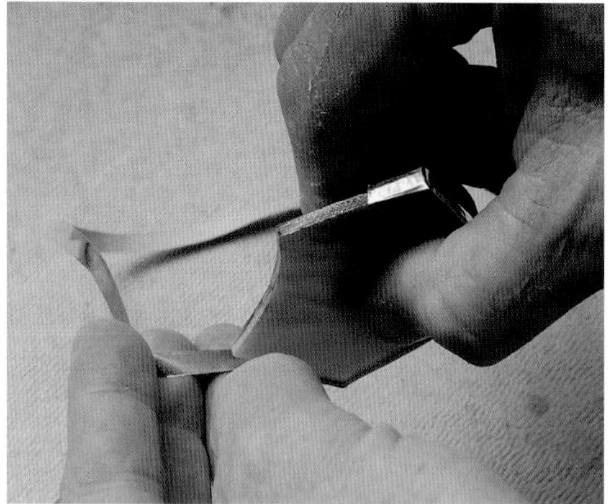

5 Trim the foil from the roll. At this point, push the foil onto the glass but not over the edges.

6 Now start in one corner of the piece. With your fingernail, fold one side under, then the other side. Fold over the adjoining edges.

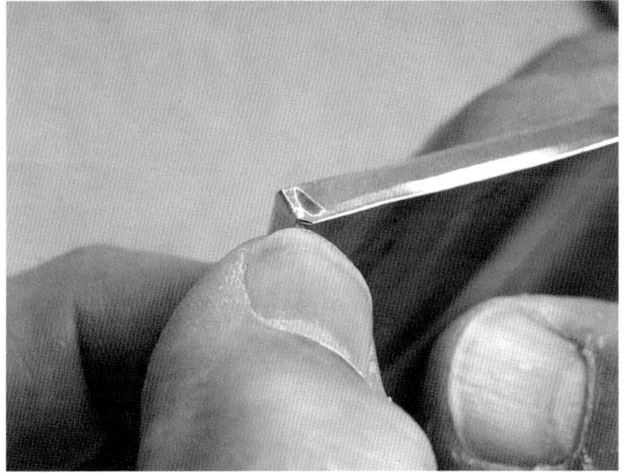

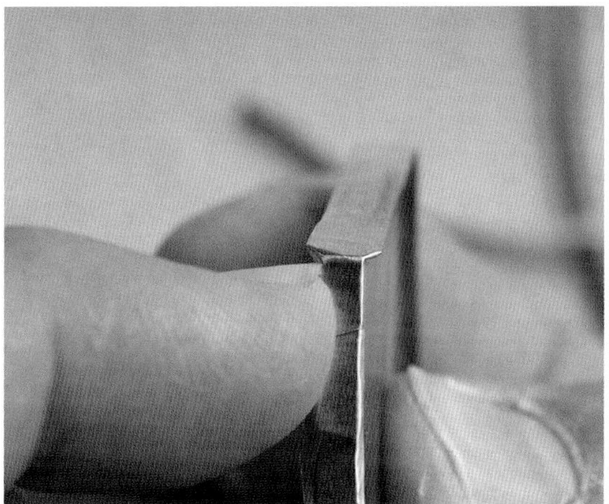

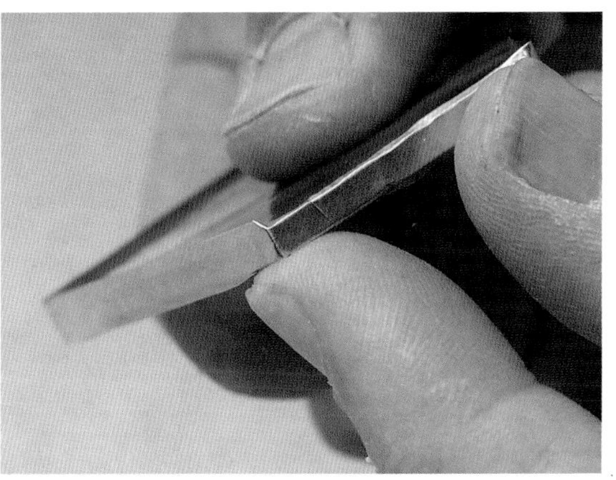

7 Do all the corners the same way, then, with two fingers, continue to press down the foil all around the piece.

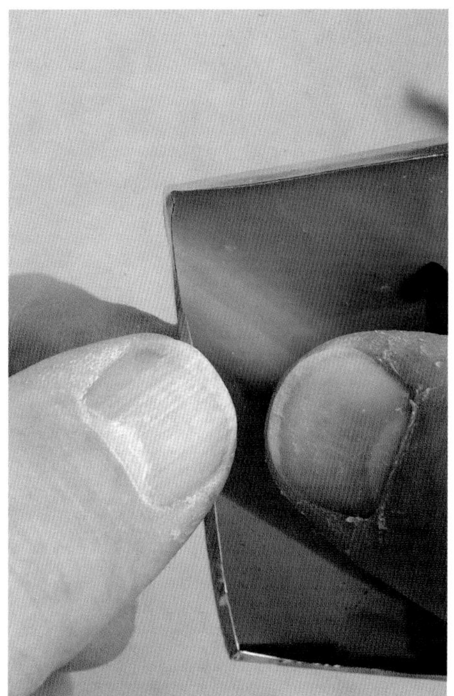

PRO TIP ✔

It's common to have some unevenness where the foil ends overlap. If that happens, trim the ends evenly with a craft knife.

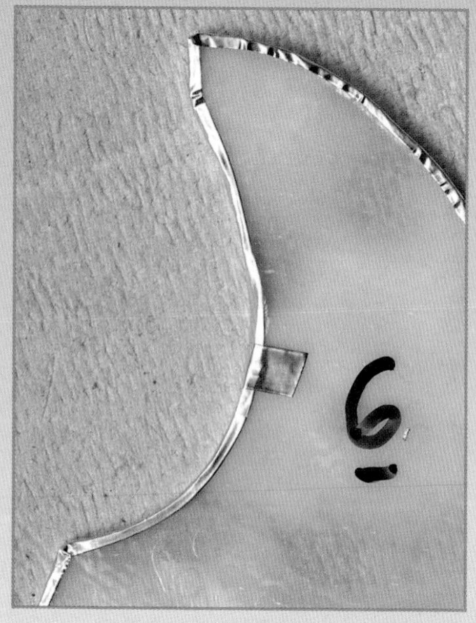

When foiling around a deep curve, the foil is likely to split when it is folded over. If that happens, wrap a short piece of foil over the split as you would place an adhesive strip across a cut. Then trim both edges evenly with a craft knife.

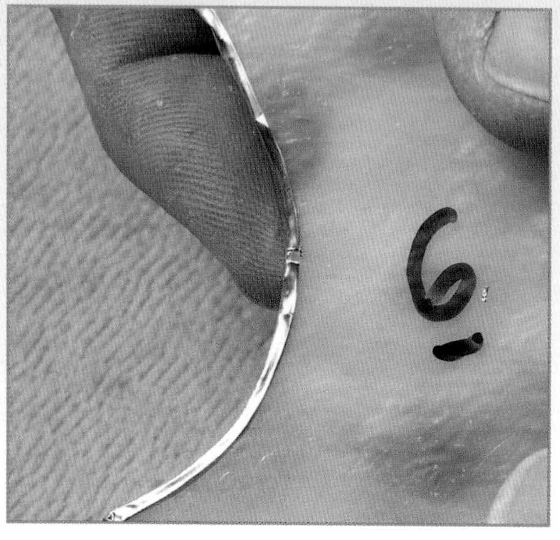

8 Using a fid, burnish the foil so that the ridges are smooth and the foil is well adhered to the glass. Turn the glass over and burnish the other side.

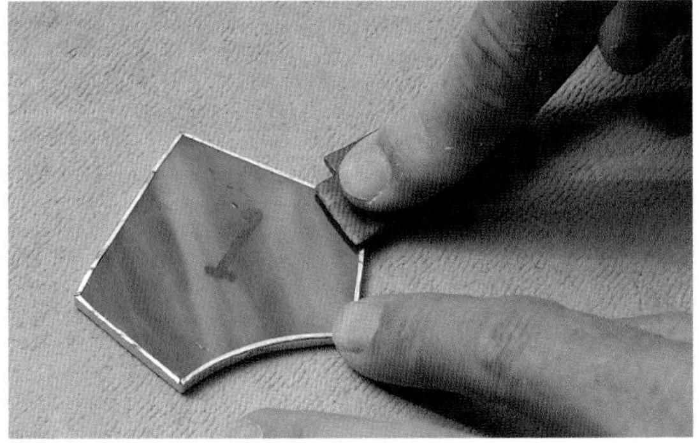

9 As you finish each piece, write its number on top and replace it on the pattern. Repeat these steps for each piece.

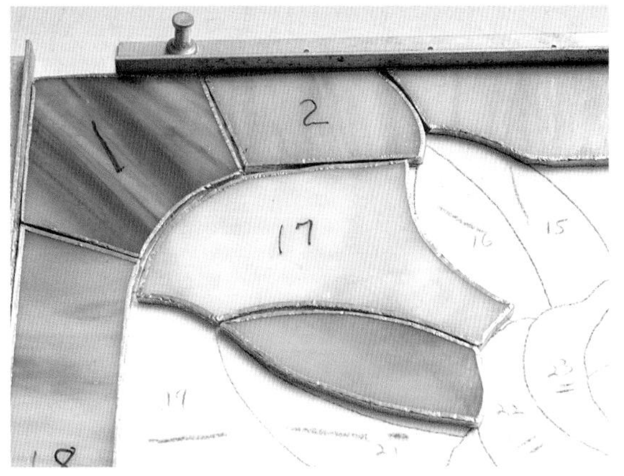

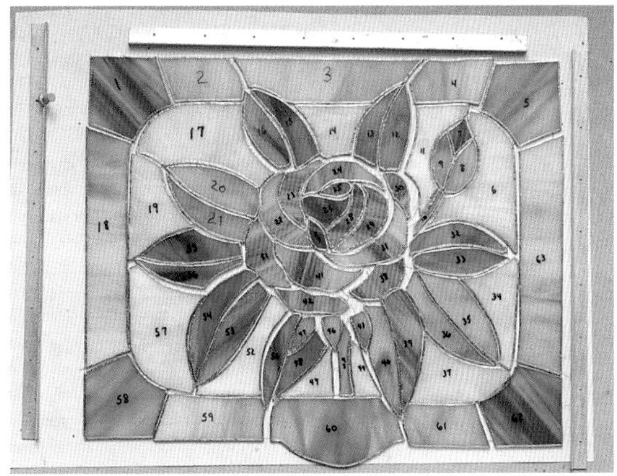

Soldering the Box Lid

To prepare for soldering the lid together, plug in your iron and set it at a suitable temperature. Remember that as you touch solder to the tip, it should melt instantly and not fall off your iron. Also, make sure to wet your cleaning sponge.

1 Attach layout strips to the three straight sides and a series of pins to the front.

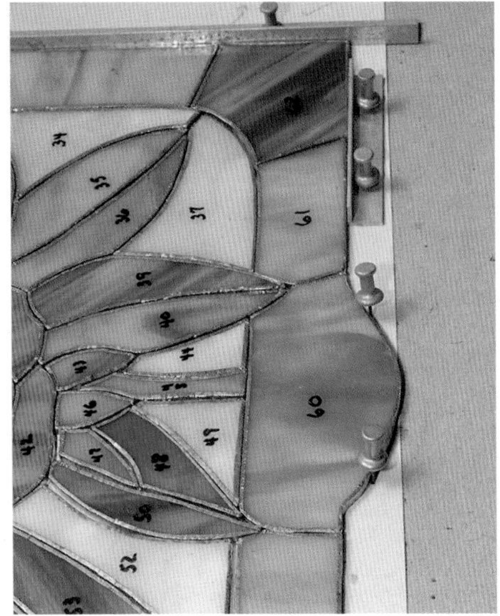

2 Again check that the lid measures 14 inches by 11 inches.

3 Flux all the copper seams.

4 If the pieces tend to shift as you apply flux, readjust them.

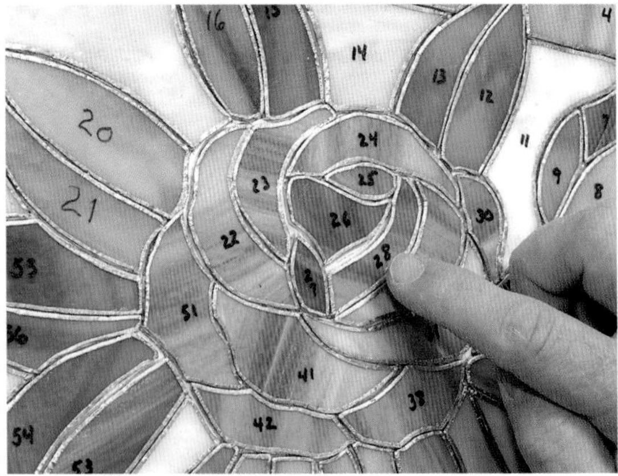

5 Begin soldering by tacking all the pieces together. Remember, at each intersection you are pinching off about $^1/_8$ inch of solder. Lift the solder out of the way, then lift the iron. Once the iron touches the solder, each tack should take about 2 seconds.

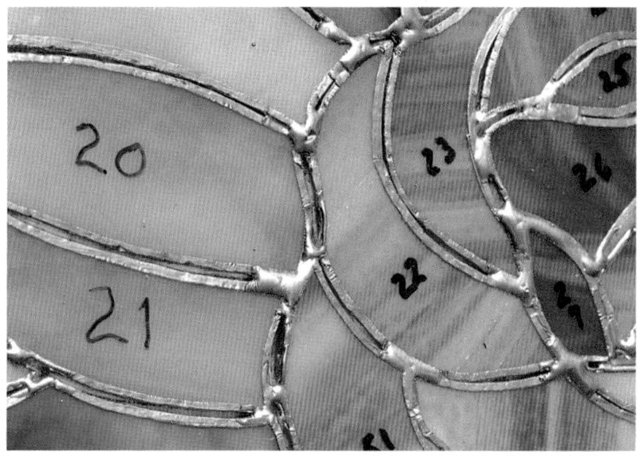

6 Remove the layout strips and pull out the pattern sheet.

7 Apply the first layer of solder to the entire panel. Remember: this first layer does not have to be perfect because another coat goes on top.

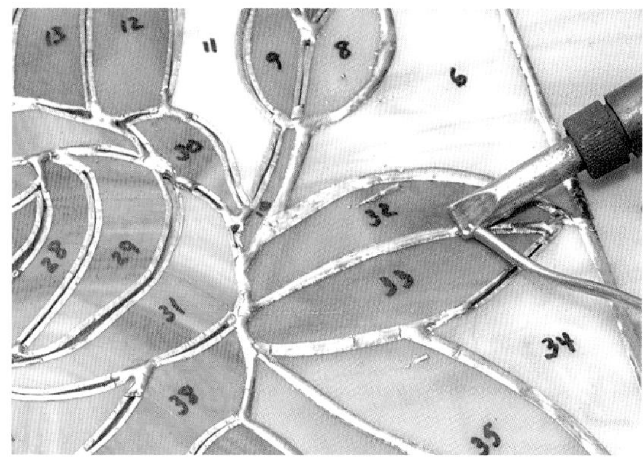

PRO TIPS ✔

If you are soldering an area where the solder is not flowing normally, you probably need to lightly reflux. You can apply flux to the top of the solder seam and then remelt the solder.

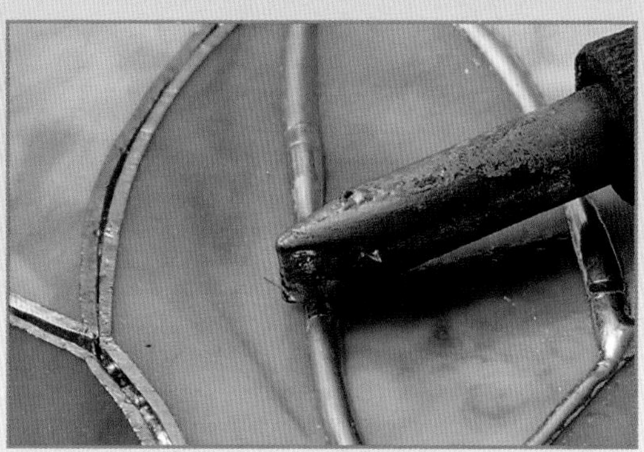

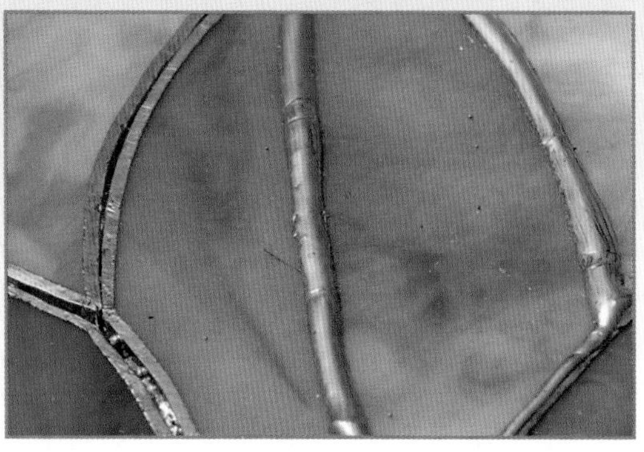

If a solder ball becomes attached to the glass, don't attempt to use the iron to melt it off. The glass could break. Dislodge the ball by pushing it firmly with the back of a flux brush.

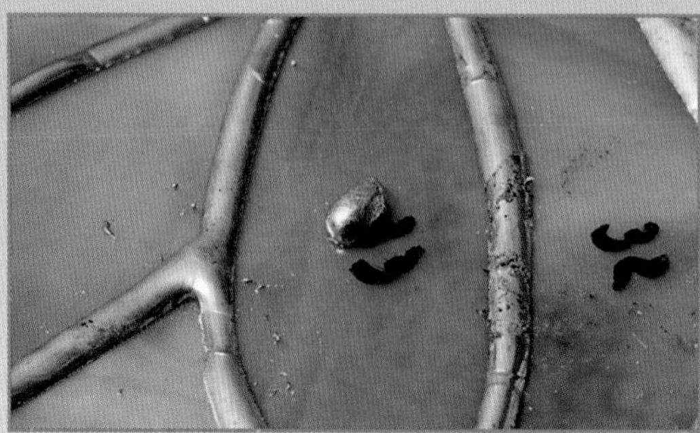

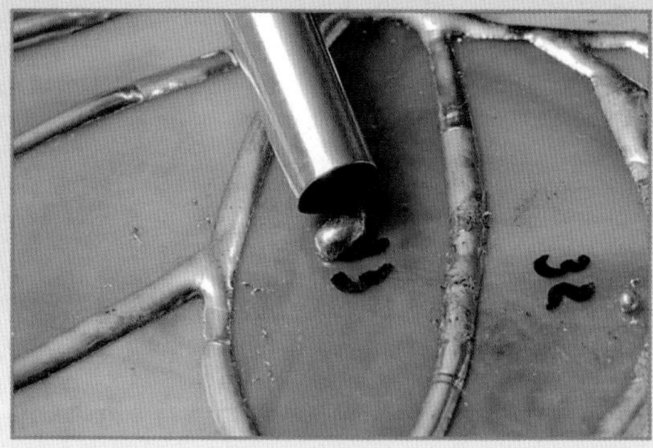

In order to keep the iron clean, wipe the tip frequently on the wet sponge in your stand.

If debris builds up on your iron tip and inhibits your ability to solder, a sal ammoniac block is the cure. Melt a small ball of solder on the block, then rub both sides of the iron tip back and forth several times. Then wipe the tip on your sponge.

8 Lightly reflux the entire panel and apply a second or beaded coat of solder.

9 Then solder the back side. Don't forget to flux first.

10 Using two notched wooden blocks, stand up the lid and flux the outside edges.

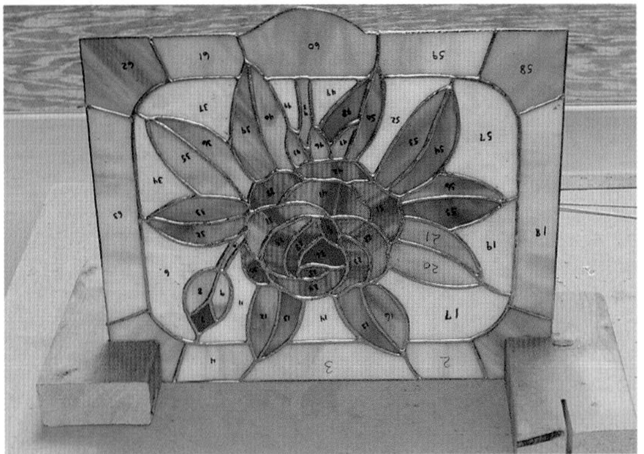

PRO TIP ✔

If you have a 1/4-inch or smaller tip for your iron, insert it now. Cool down your iron first!

11 Apply a slightly rounded bead of solder to the outer edges. Instead of resting the whole tip of the iron on the foil, try using just the point. By building up the solder a bit, the edges will stiffen and are less likely to pull loose.

12 When you reach the front with the rounded edge, prop one side on the top of a block to help level that part of the edge. You will only be able to solder about 1/2 inch at a time before you'll need to readjust the angle.

13 Lay the lid flat and lightly coat the overlapped edges that might not be covered yet.

14 Wash and dry the finished box top and set it aside. It's okay to admire your work!

Cutting the Box Parts

1 It's important that the sides of the box be cut straight so they are level and will line up properly with the lid. A glass square has a lip that allows it to be placed on a straight edge of glass, ensuring a 90-degree cut.

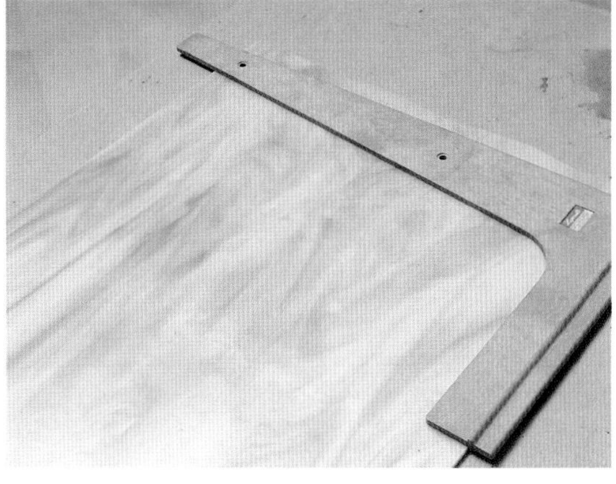

2 Before cutting strips for the box sides, be certain that you start with a squared edge, one that has a true 90-degree angle. To do that, place the square against a straight edge on the glass and see if the edge, which is at a 90-degree angle, is straight.

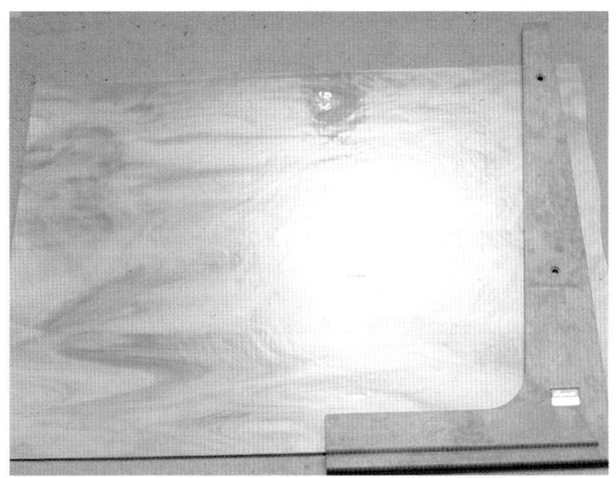

If not, then cut off about $^{1}/_{2}$ inch. Running pliers work well for this.

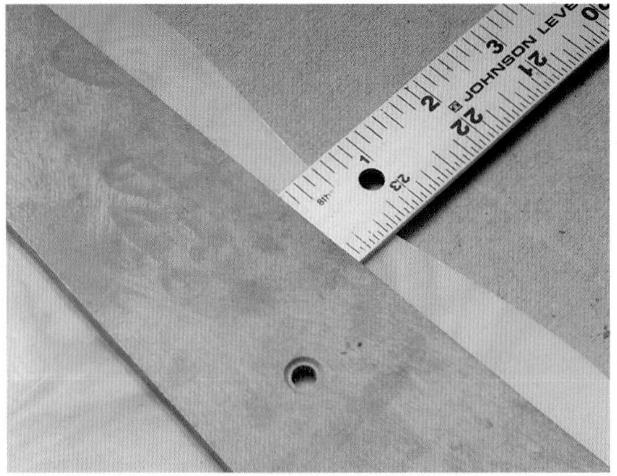

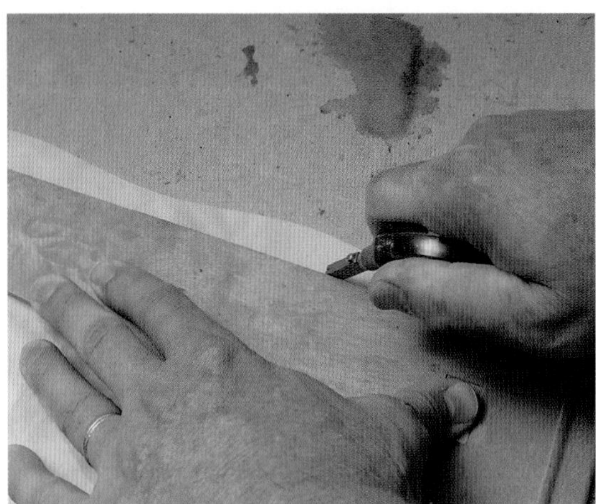

3 There will often be burrs of glass left behind after the strips are broken. Take these off with a carborundum stone or electric grinder.

For all parts of the box bottom, as well as the lip that gets attached to the lid, we have indicated sizes as well as actual templates (see page 129) for cutting the glass. If you are versed in reading a ruler, you can avoid paper patterns for these pieces.

Ideally, the length of glass you want to work with should be 14 inches or longer. Decide the color grain direction you want for the box sides.

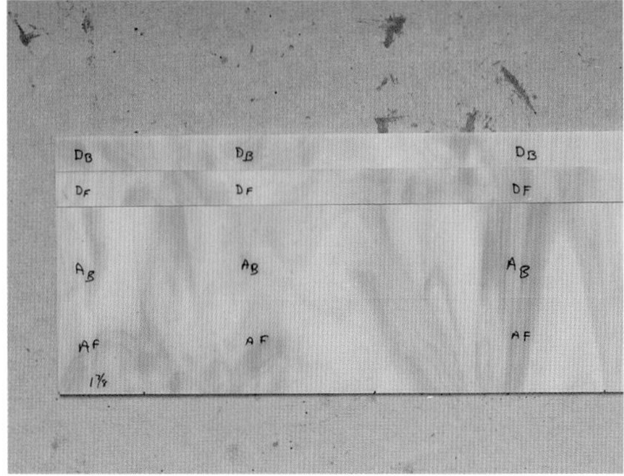

The four sides of the box (A and B) are 2 inches high.

4 Measure 2 inches and place a dot at that point on the glass.

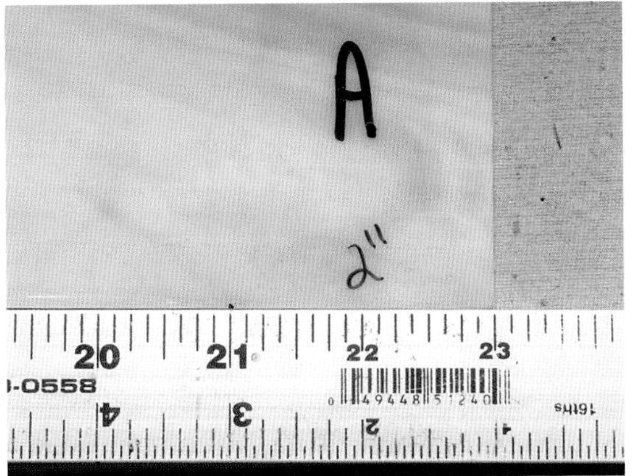

5 Place the glass square on the bottom edge of the glass and line up your cutter wheel with the dot. Cut four strips, each 2 inches wide, and mark two strips A and two strips B.

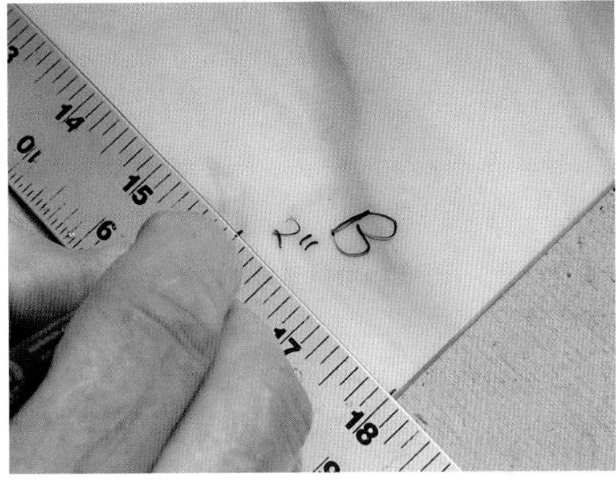

6 Now measure $^{3}/_{4}$ inch on the glass and cut four strips for the pieces that will form the lip of the box top (C and D).

7 Attach a metal layout block to your work board and place the two A strips and two D strips against it. Be sure that the long edges of the strips are aligned against each other.

8 Measure the bottom piece at 13 11/16 inches and place a dot at that point.

9 Use the square to cut off the excess glass.

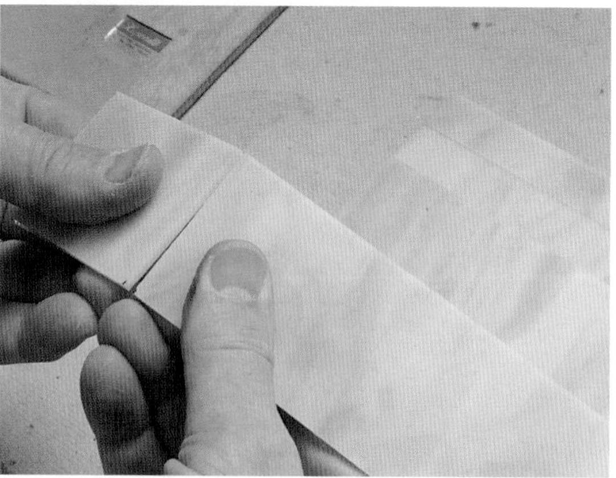

10 Replace the strips against the layout block. Measure, then place dots at $1^7/_8$ inches from both ends.

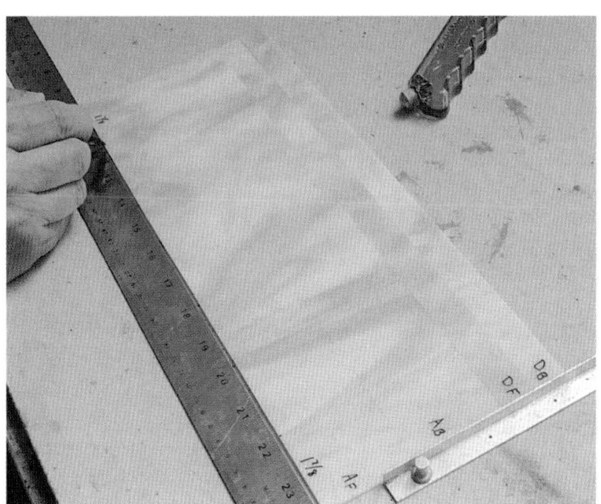

11 Measure and place a dot 5 inches from either of the other two dots. This placement will be very close to the middle of the strip.

12 In order to keep all the pieces from each section together, you'll want to code them. On the A strip closest to you, mark the four sections with AF (A front). The second A section is designated AB (A back). The first D section is DF (D front), and the second D section is DB (D back).

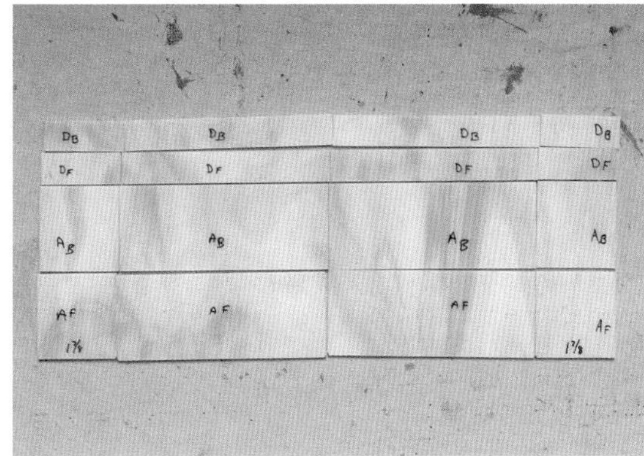

13 Using the glass square, line up your cutter at the first dot. Score across the four strips and break all four pieces.

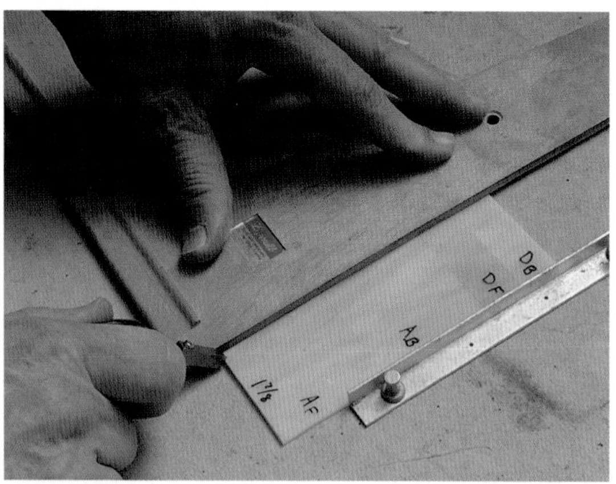

14 Rearrange the pieces in their original order.

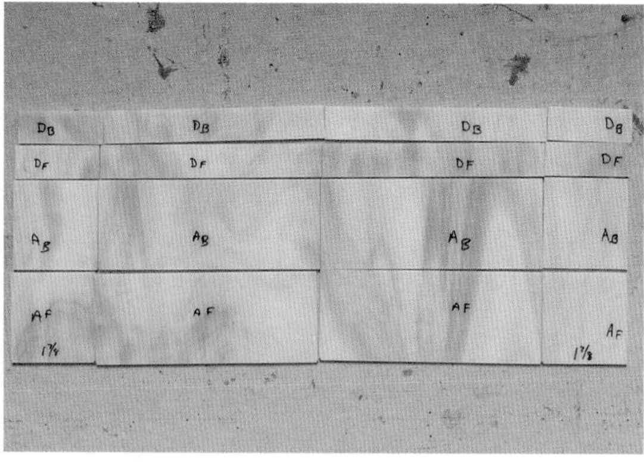

15 Align the remaining four strips against the layout block. Measure the bottom glass strip 10 11/16 inches from the layout block and put a dot at that point.

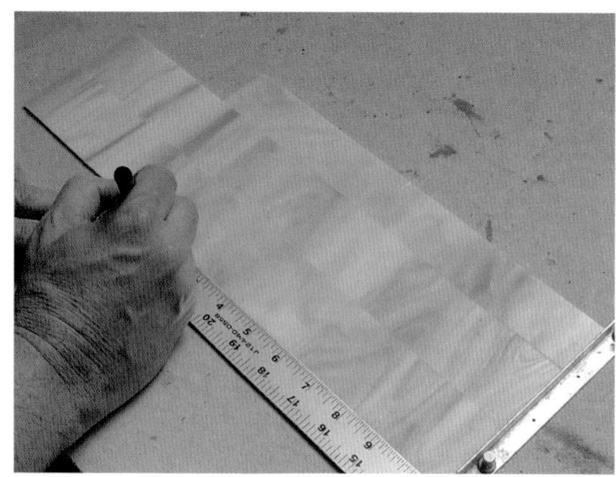

16 Cut off the excess.

17 Measure the strips at 1 7/8 inches from the left and right and put dots at those locations.

18 Again, using the glass square, cut the four strips at the dots. Break all the pieces.

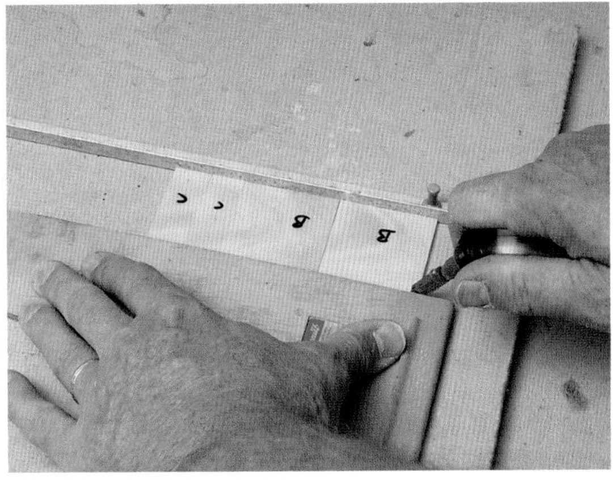

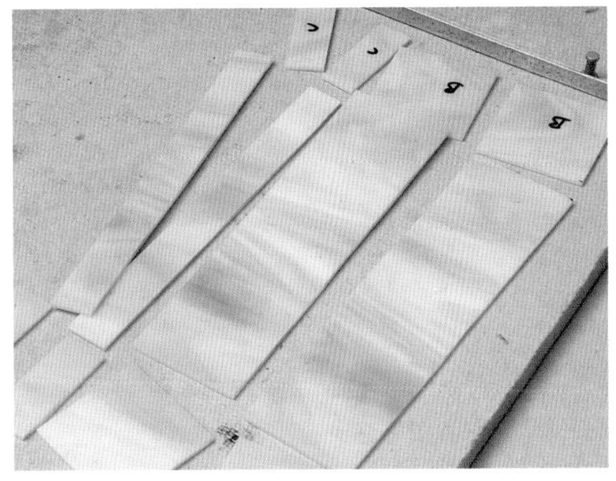

19 Write BL (B left) on the four pieces that make up the first B strip. This strip will be the left side of the box. Write BR (B right) on the second B strip pieces. Finish by writing CL on the pieces for the first C strip pieces and CR on the second C strip pieces.

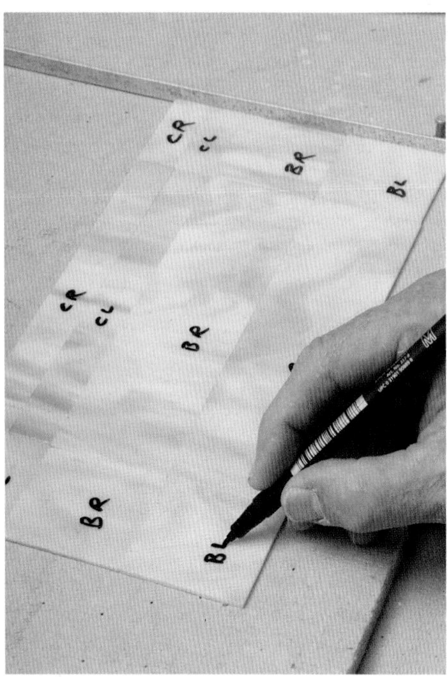

Cutting the Mirror Bottom

Before you go about cutting the mirror for the bottom of the box, brush your work board thoroughly and put down a protective piece of paper, such as newspaper. If you end up scratching the back of the mirror with an invisible speck of glass, the scratch is there for life, so be careful.

1 With your cutting square, check that the mirror is square. If not, trim off about $^1/_2$ inch to give it a straight edge.

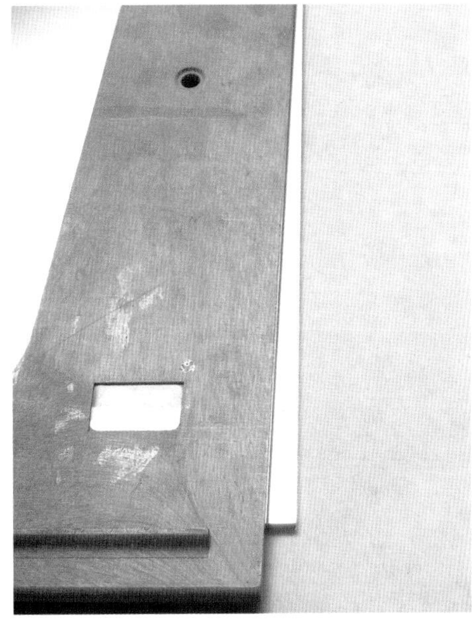

2 Measure and cut the mirror at 14 inches. Then turn and cut it at 11 inches (the same measurements as the box lid).

3 Remove any sharp flares or burrs with a stone or grinder, being careful not to chip the backing.

4 Wash and dry the mirror. Place it reflective side down on a clean piece of paper. You don't want to scratch the front of the mirror either!

5 The silvering on the mirror that makes it reflective can react adversely to flux and patina, causing the silvering to corrode. This "creeping black" is frequently seen in old mirrors.

Spraying the edges of the mirror with a protector will prevent this problem. Spray at an angle so the edges where the glass and backing meet are covered. Spray about 1 inch toward the center of the mirror. Apply three coats, allowing a 15-minute drying time between each coat.

6 Set the bottom aside until later.

Attaching the Lip to the Box Top

1 Remove any burrs from the pieces that make up the lip of the box top (C and D). Wash and foil.

2 It is now time to solder the sections. A small tip for your iron will be handy for this.

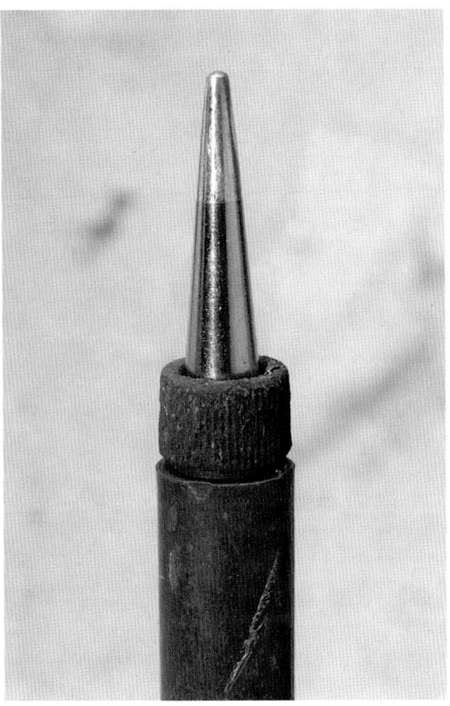

3 Along a metal layout strip, align, in order, the four pieces that make up the DF section. Secure the pieces with pins, setting them tightly together. Attach a second layout strip along the top.

4 Solder the seams. Remove the piece from the jig and solder the back seams.

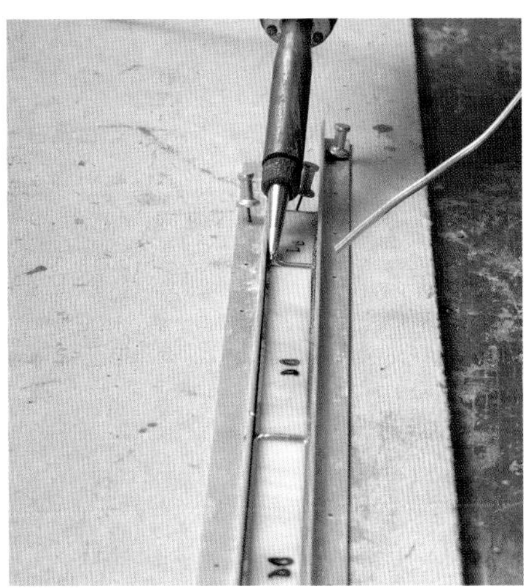

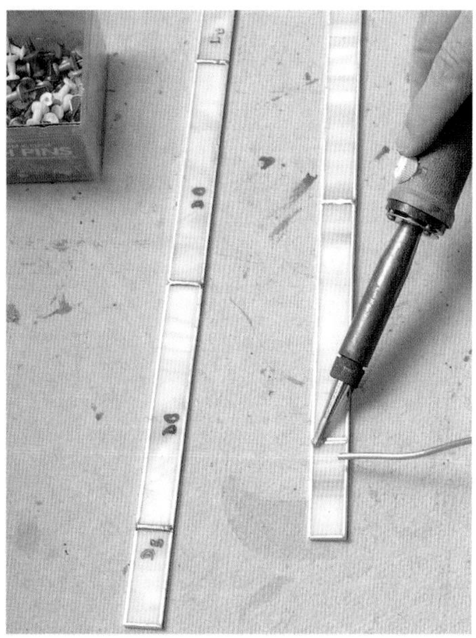

5 Repeat the same steps for the DB section and the two C sections.

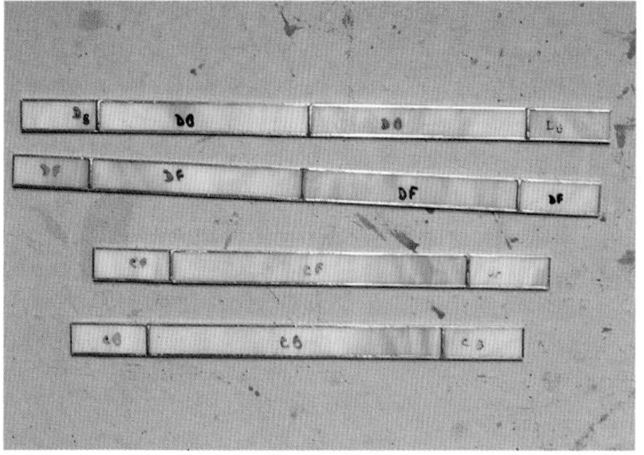

6 Stand each soldered section between two metal strips, flux, and apply a thin coat of solder to the outside edges.

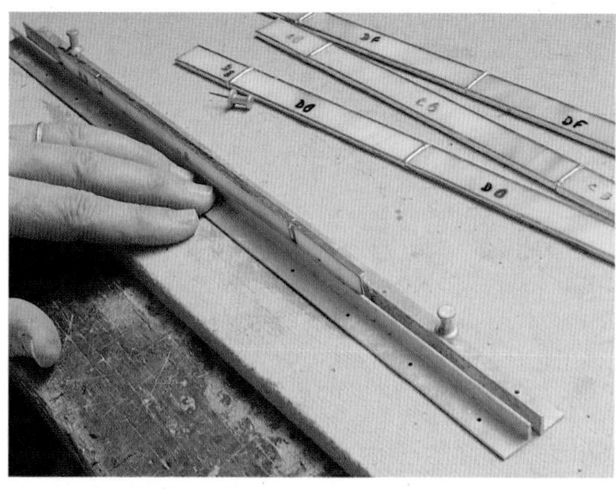

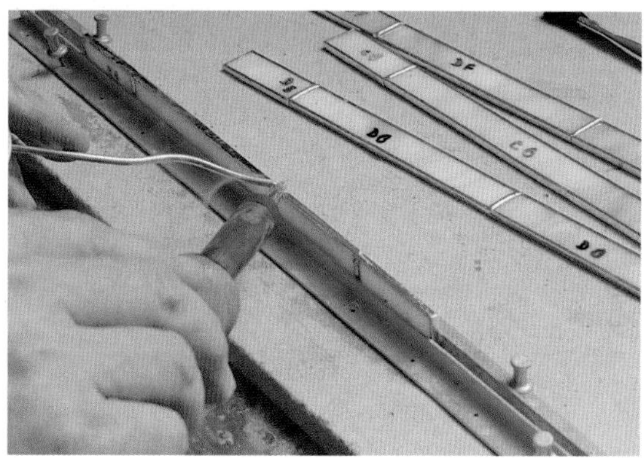

7 Lay the strips flat and solder the front and back edges.

8 Turn the box lid upside down with the rear of the design closest to you. Set the DB section on the edge of the lid. It should be flush with the edge of the lid and centered so that it sits back from both lid sides about $^{1}/_{8}$ inch.

9 Flux the long seam on the outside and tack-solder the three spots where the vertical seams from the lip meet the lid.

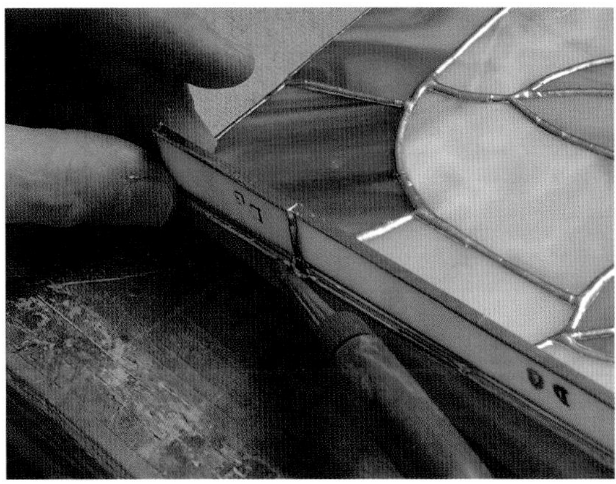

10 Repeat steps 8 and 9 for the other three sections.

11 The corners formed by two lip sections should meet at the inside edges.

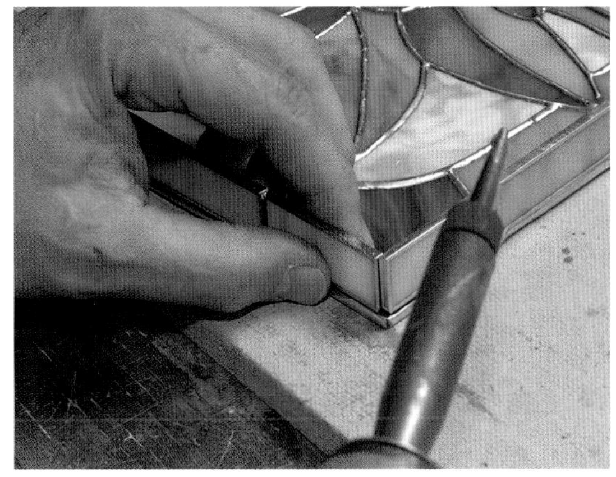

12 Tack-solder that area as well.

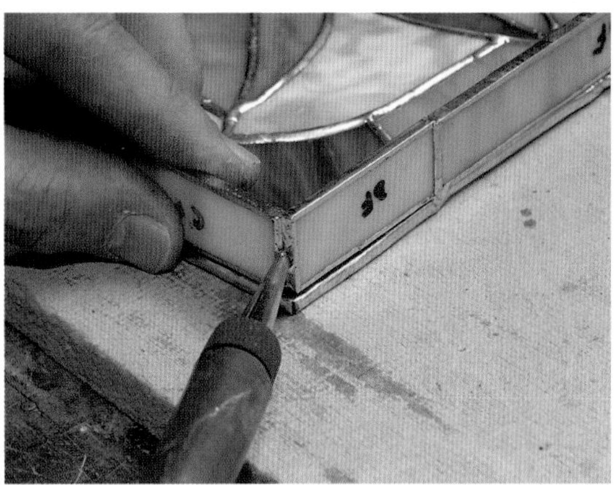

13 Also attach the lip to the box top at all inside points where seams from the lid meet the lip.

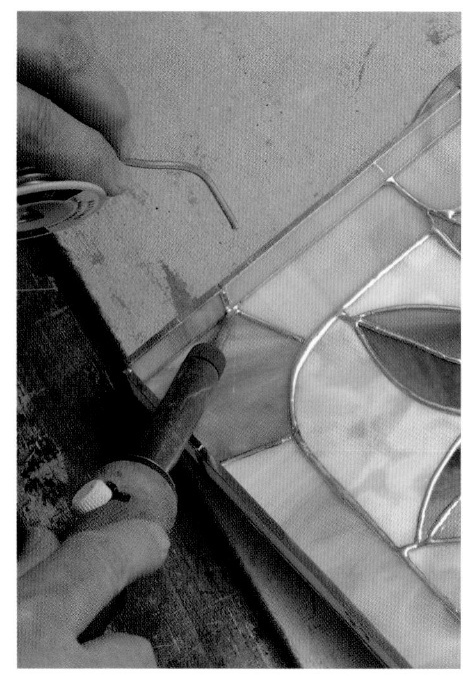

14 Lean the lid against a sturdy box for support, and apply a raised bead of solder to the four long seams and the four corners.

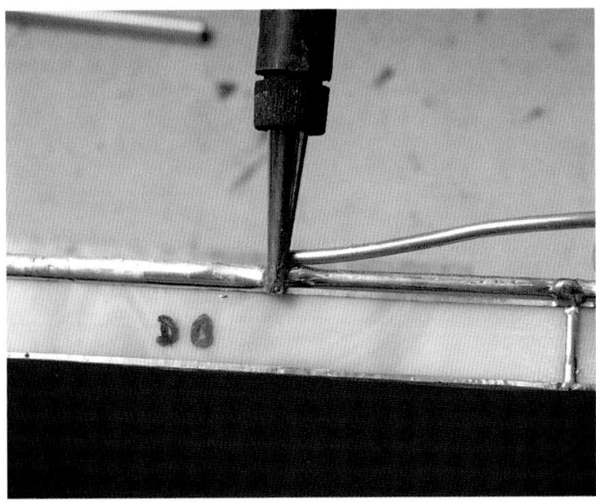

PRO TIP ✔

Flat-solder each seam first, then finish with a beaded coat. This step will help prevent solder from melting through.

15 Lay the lid on your table and apply a raised bead of solder to the lip edges. Turn the lid on end and tin any remaining areas that are not yet covered with solder.

Building the Box Sides and Bottom

1 Lay out the pieces for the A and B sections the same way you did for the box top lip sections. Solder the pieces for each section together.

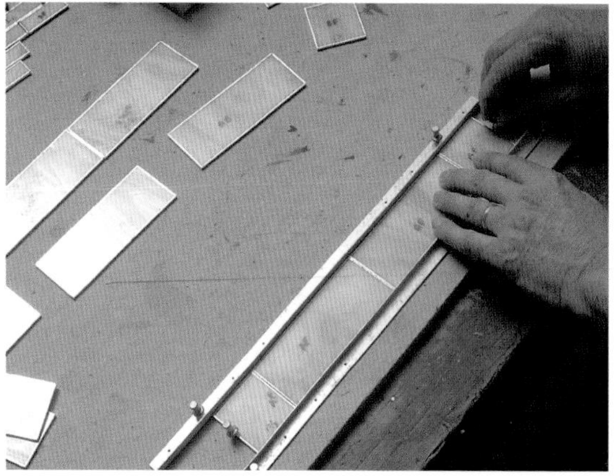

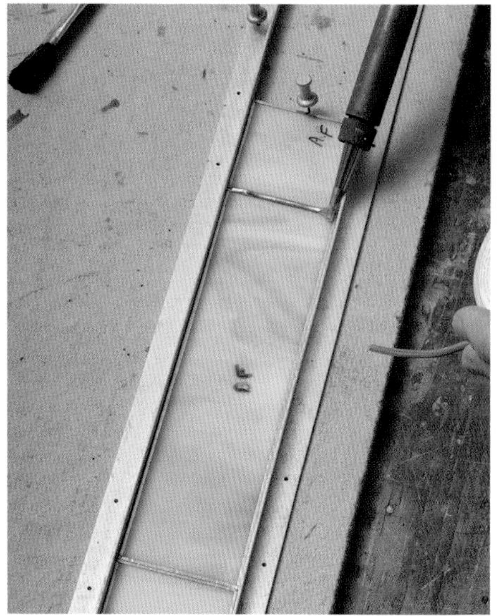

2 Insert one end of the AF section into a notched wood block. Do the same for the right side BR section. Position them at a 90-degree angle to each other.

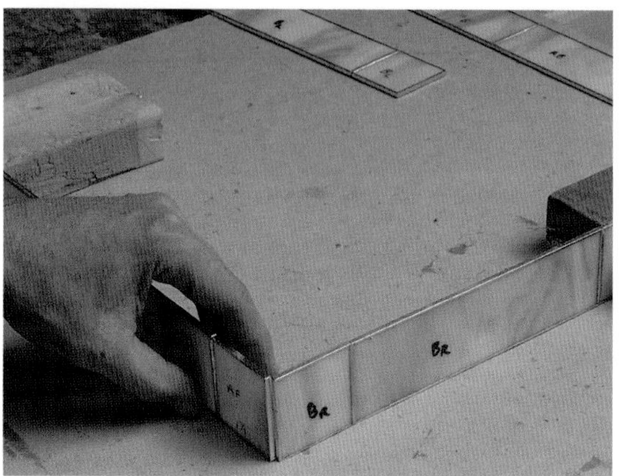

3 The inside vertical edges should touch each other.

PRO TIP ✔

There will frequently be times when you want to hold pieces of glass steady as you solder them. Instead of holding the solder spool, place it on your work board in close proximity to the area to be soldered. This will free up your hand to position pieces accurately.

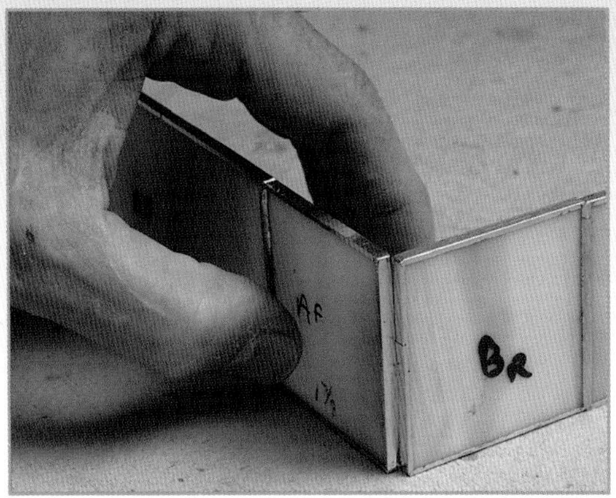

Cool your iron on the wet sponge for 2 to 3 seconds. Melt off a small amount of solder, keeping it attached to the iron tip, and transfer it to the area to be soldered.

4 Flux this seam, then tack-solder top and bottom.

5 Remove one of the blocks and insert the back section (AB) into it. Attach it to a side section the same way, again with the inside edges touching.

6 Place the BL (left) section of the box in place and hold it there by placing wood blocks on both sides. Flux and tack-solder both ends. Remember to line up the inside edges at the corners.

7 Flux the top edges and melt a thin coat of solder all around.

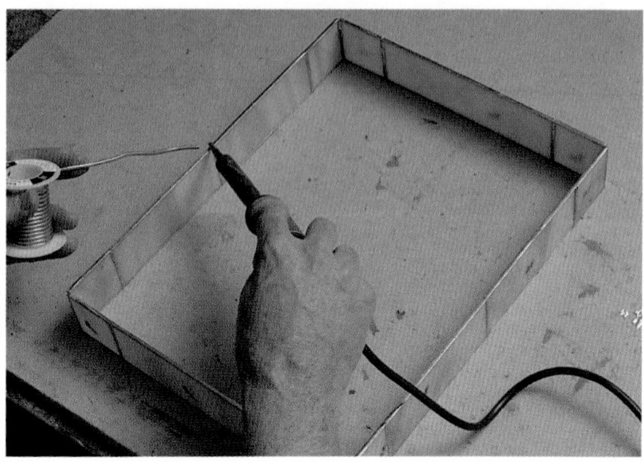

8 Carefully turn the box side unit on end and tin the overlapped edges, top and bottom. Support the unit with your other hand because it will be very wobbly at this point. When finished, place the unit back on the work surface with the soldered edge up.

9 Foil the mirror bottom. Flux and tin the edge that overlaps onto the reflective side. If you don't do this step, you might get some copper reflection when the bottom is attached.

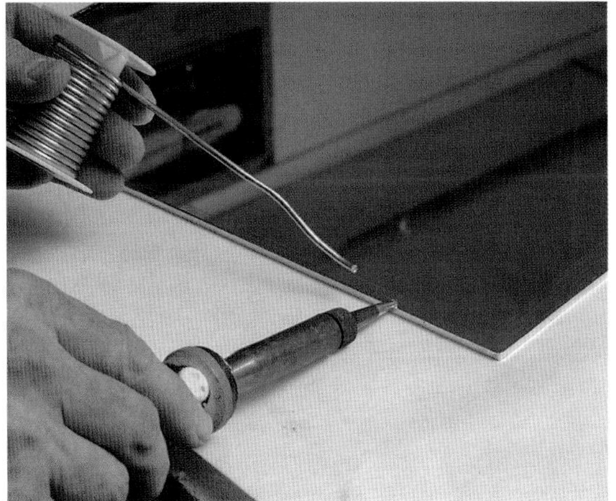

10 Place the mirror bottom on top of the four sides.

11 With your hands on opposite sides, feel that the sides are even with the bottom. Adjust the sides until the mirror and sides are even all around.

12 Check the corners as well.

13 Hold the mirror so that it does not move and flux the sides' bottom seams all around.

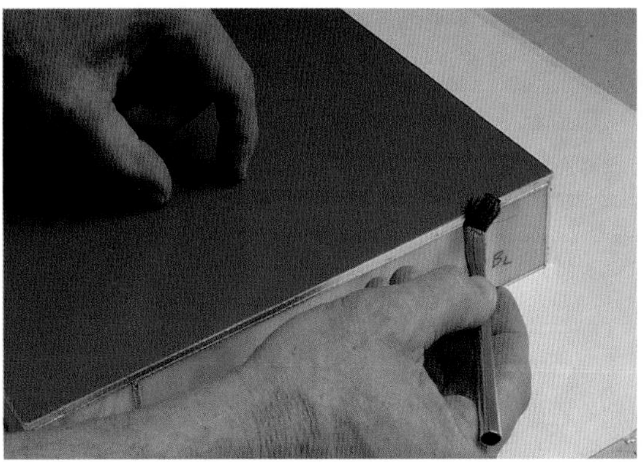

14 Continue holding the mirror in place and tack-solder the mirror at two points on each of the four edges.

15 The box bottom is now stable enough to move. Stand the box up against a cardboard box or wooden blocks and finish soldering the bottom seams.

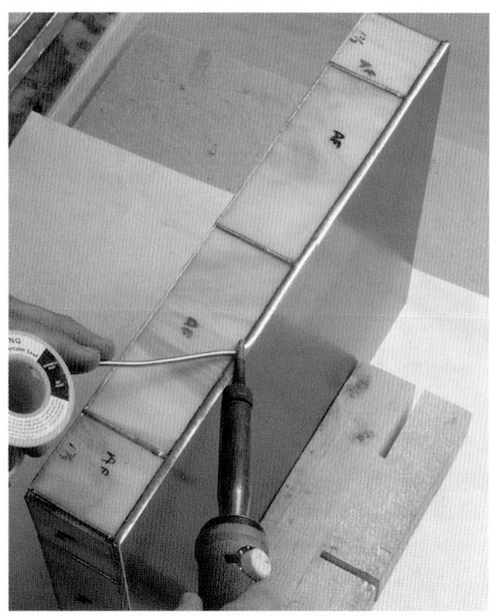

16 Prop one end of the box on a wood block, then solder the corner. First apply a base coat and then a beaded coat. Repeat this step for the other three corners.

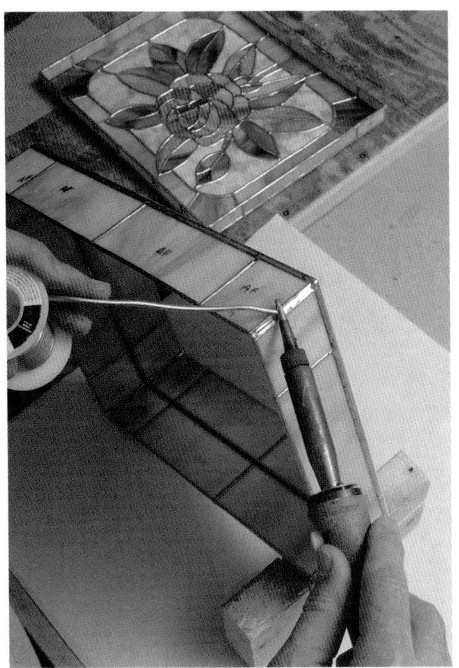

17 Place the box mirror side down and put a raised bead of solder on the top edges of the box. This step will stiffen the foil to reduce the possibility of it lifting off the box.

18 Tin the overlapped edges, top and bottom.

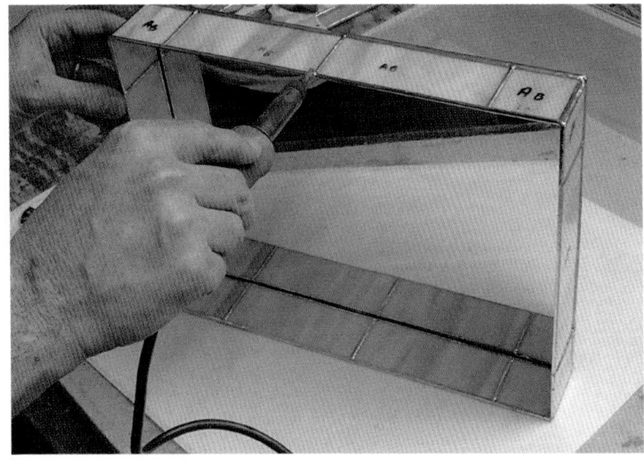

19 All the copper on the box should now be covered. Do a quick check to see.

20 Now wash and dry the assembled box bottom.

Attaching the Shelf, Dividers, and Brace System

Now you should cut strips for the long back brace (G) and three short braces (J). These are all 3/4 inch wide.

1 Measure the inside length of the box to verify that it is 13 11/16 inches.

2 Measure and cut G accordingly.

PRO TIP ✔

A thumb square is handy for cutting strips to length. To make one, purchase an inexpensive plastic square and cut off the ends. The one pictured here is 2 inches wide by 3 inches high.

3 Check to see that it fits: A little short at this point is okay.

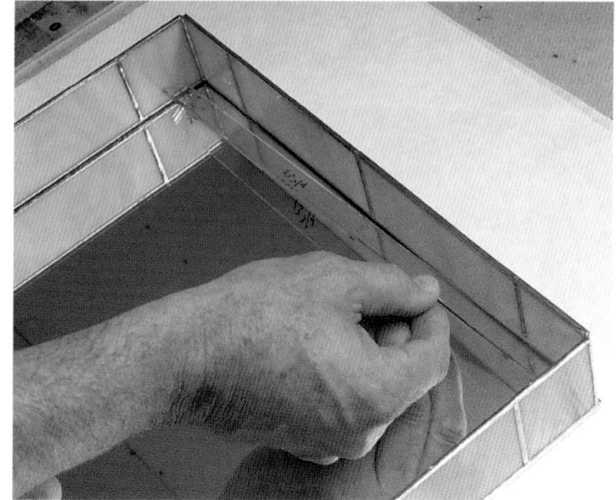

4 Cut the three short braces (J) $1^5/8$ inches long.

5 Foil, flux, and tin all four braces. Clean the braces—access to them is not possible once the shelf is in place.

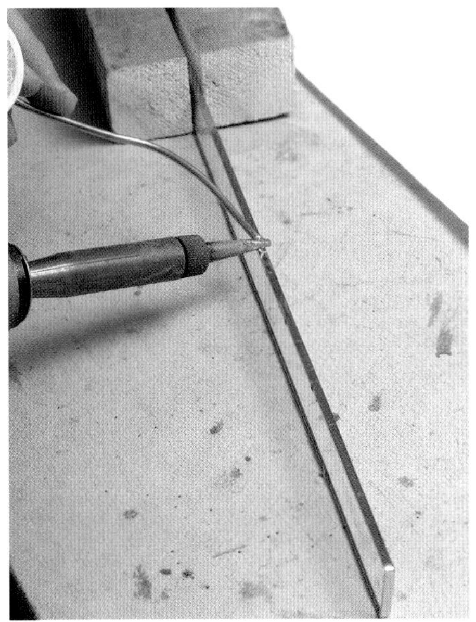

6 Set brace G against the back of the box, making sure it sits flat on the mirror. Apply a little flux, and tack-solder at the three seams on the back of the box and in both corners. Use solder sparingly. If the solder protrudes up too much, the shelf will not be flat. If there are any high spots of solder, flux and smooth them out.

7 Clean off the flux.

8 Attach the short braces. The one in the middle will be soldered where it meets brace G, top and bottom. The braces on the ends get soldered against brace G, top and bottom, and also at the opposite ends where they meet the first soldered seam on the box sides. Again, you do not need much flux or solder.

9 Cut the shelf strip (F) at 1 3/4 inches.

10 Measure the other inside length of the box to verify that it is 13 11/16 inches. Cut the shelf to fit, modifying it if necessary.

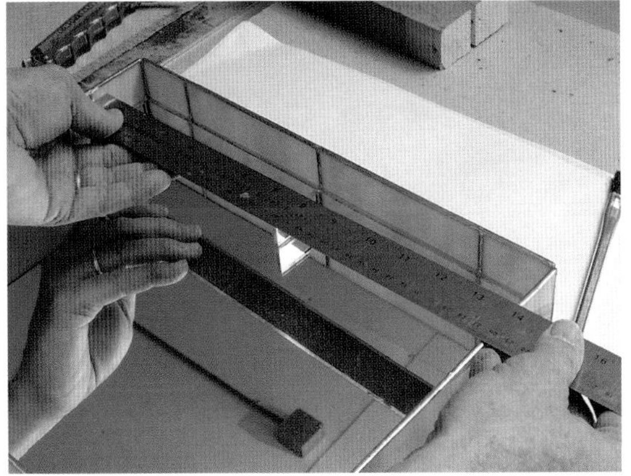

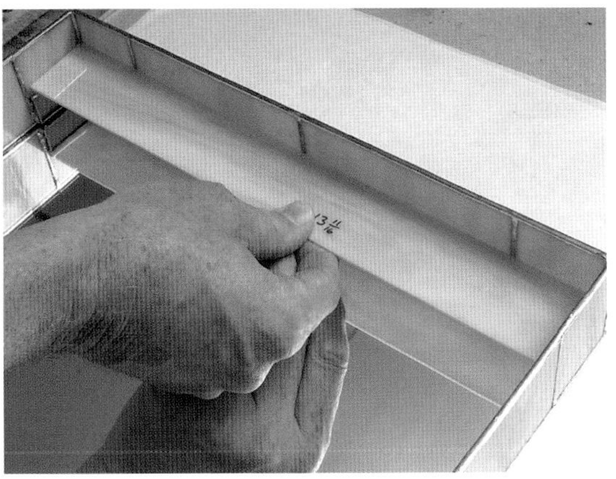

11 Grind as necessary, wash, foil, and tin.

12 Cut the shelf front pieces (E1 and E2). Start with a strip 1 3/4 inches wide.

13 Cut out paper templates for both pieces, and use rubber cement to attach them to the glass.

14 Cut out the pieces and check that they fit; wash and foil.

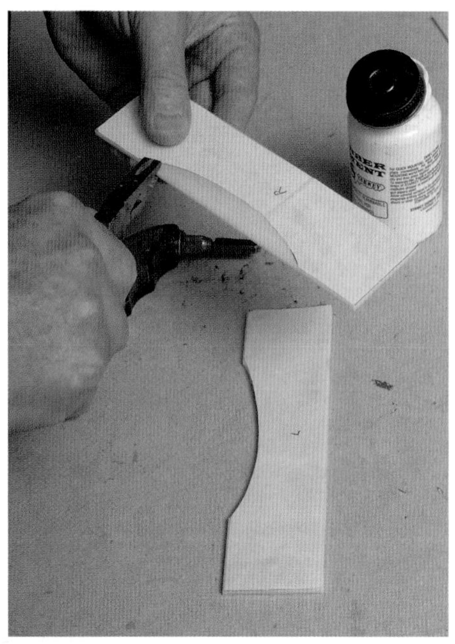

15 Place the two pieces along a layout strip. Insert pushpins at both ends and solder the pieces together.

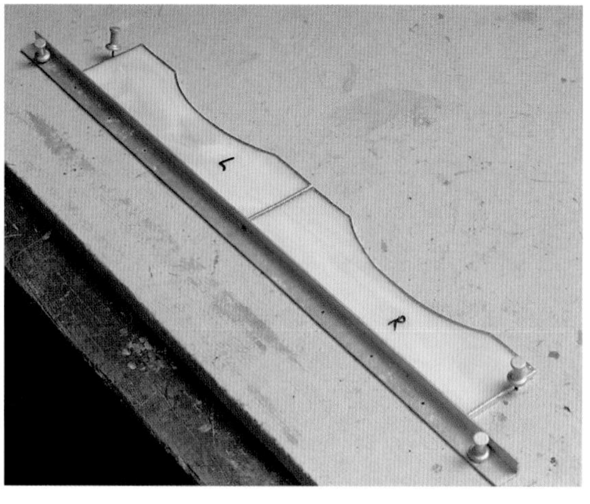

16 Tin the sides and bottom. Bead-solder the top. Wash and dry the shelf and the shelf front.

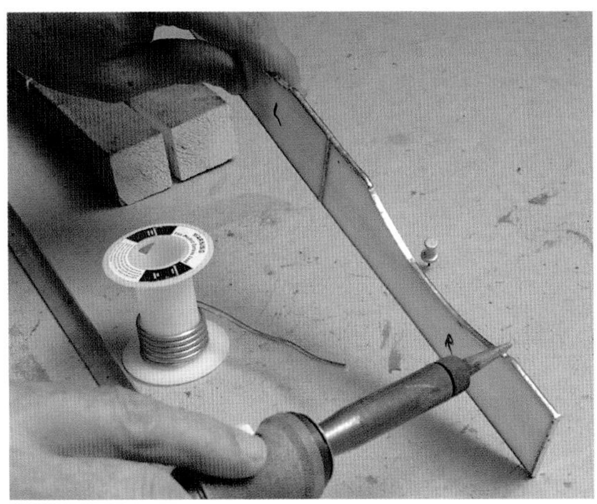

17 Place the shelf on the braces and solder where it meets the three short braces in front and the five seams on the back of the box. Again, only use a little solder.

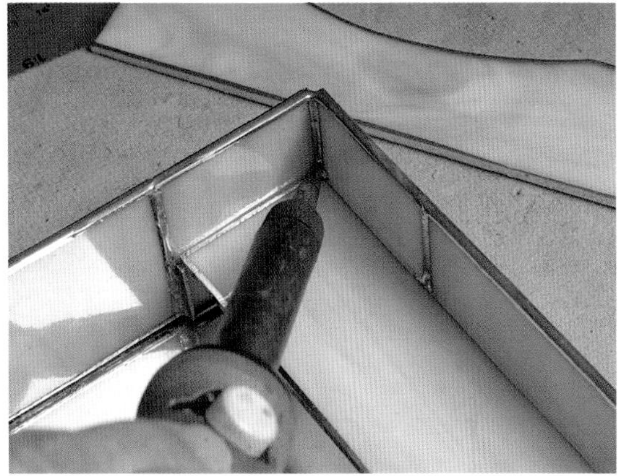

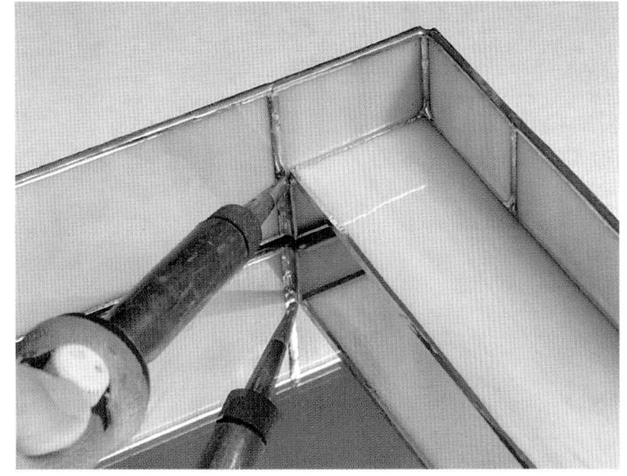

18 Clean the flux from those areas.

19 Set the shelf front against the shelf and short braces. Solder it, top and bottom, at the seams on the box sides and where it meets the shelf at the ends and middle.

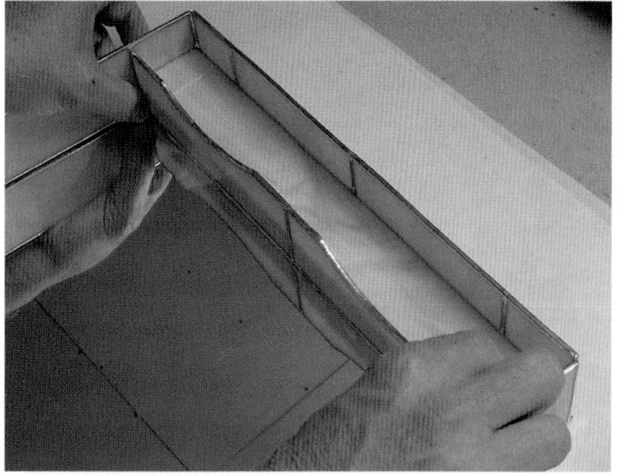

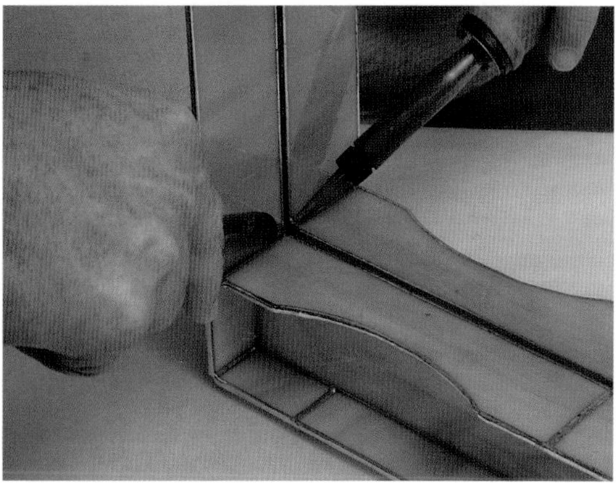

20 Clean off the flux.

21 Cut the box divider (H). Start with a 2-inch strip and cement a paper template to it. Finish cutting. Measure for fit.

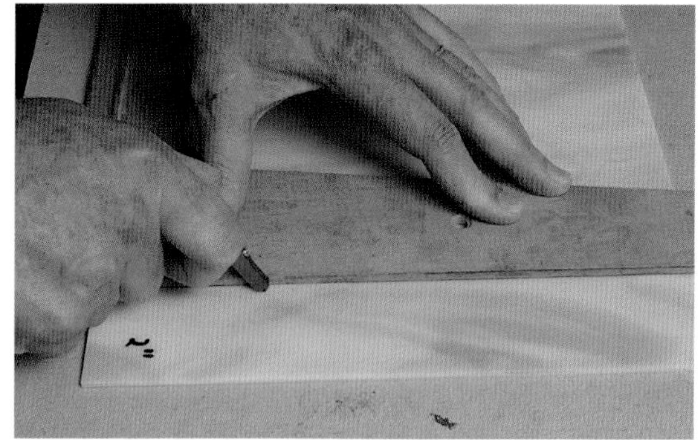

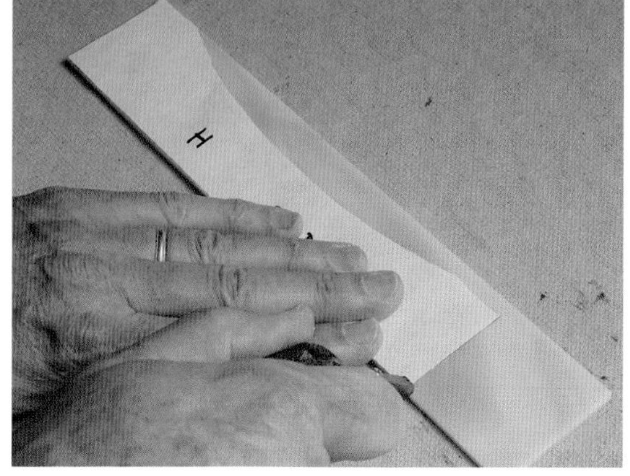

22 Grind, wash, foil, flux, and tin the divider. Put a beaded coat on the top. This step will stiffen the foil, preventing it from lifting due to an inadvertent fingernail. Wash and dry.

23 Place the divider between the shelf and the front of the box at their center seams.

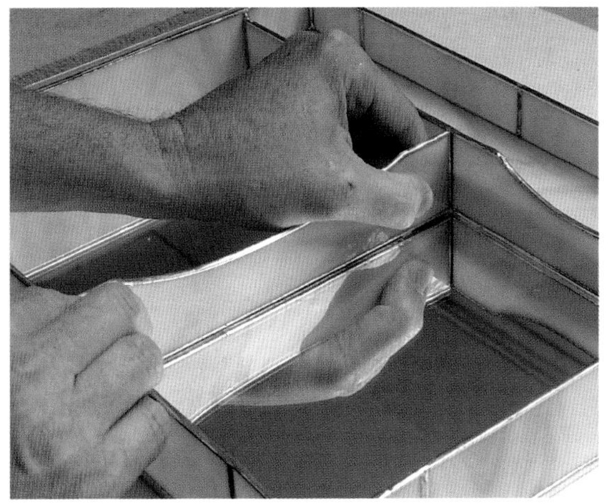

24 Solder both ends, top and bottom.

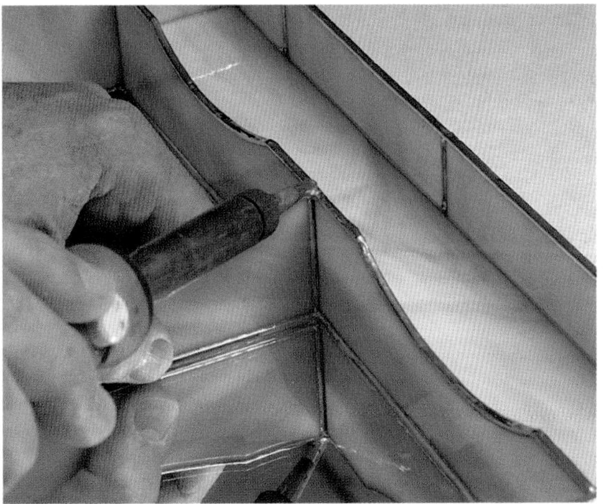

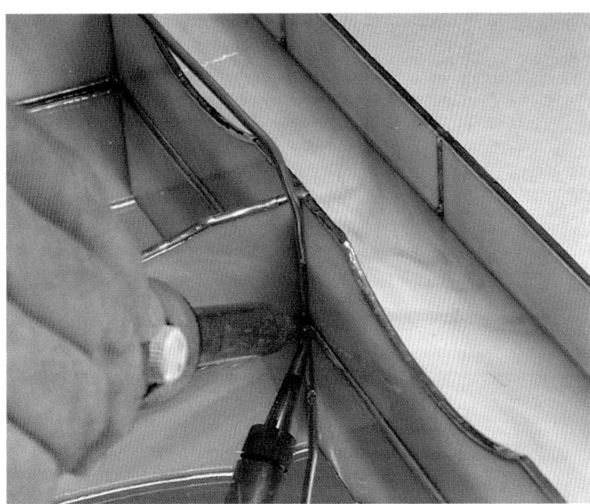

25 Cut the shelf divider (I) and check it for fit. Grind, wash, foil, and tin. Solder at the shelf midpoint and middle seam of the back of the box. Be sure to attach it at the top and bottom.

26 Wash off the flux.

Cutting and Assembling the Box Feet

For the box feet, you will need to cut eight pieces. Start with a 2-inch strip.

1 Because you have multiple repeat cuts, making a sturdy template will help. Take a piece of window glass, cut an accurate template, and grind the piece smooth.

2 Place the template on the glass strip as shown and draw a line along the curve.

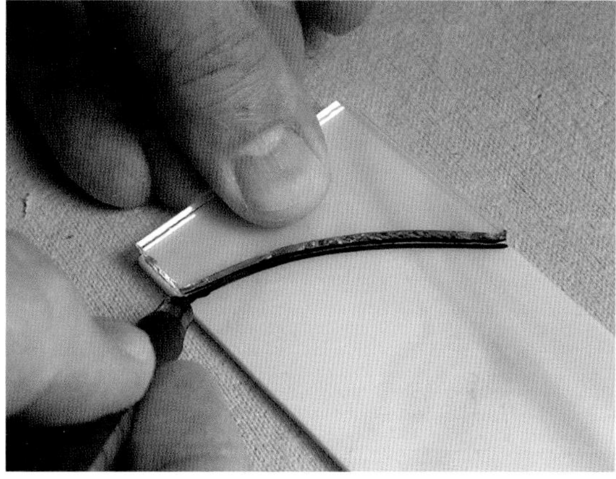

3 Cut on the inside of the line. The marker line will be on the waste glass.

4 Square the strip in preparation for the next piece.

5 After you have cut four leg pieces, turn your template over so you can make reversed, or mirror image, cuts. Cut four of these.

6 After foiling the pieces, put one left leg piece at a right angle to a right leg piece. Secure them with layout strips on both sides of both leg parts. The inside edges should be touching.

7 Flux and tack-solder. Repeat for the three remaining legs.

8 Solder the inside seams.

9 Solder the outside seams by propping each so it is horizontal. Your glass cutter can be used as a prop.

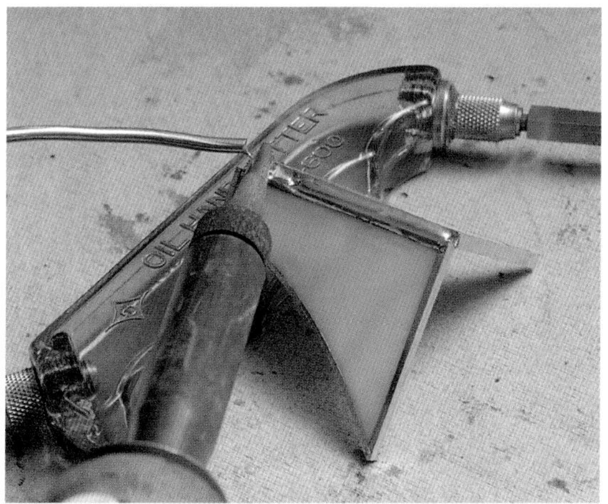

10 Tin the top and bottom edges and put a beaded coat of solder on the curved edges.

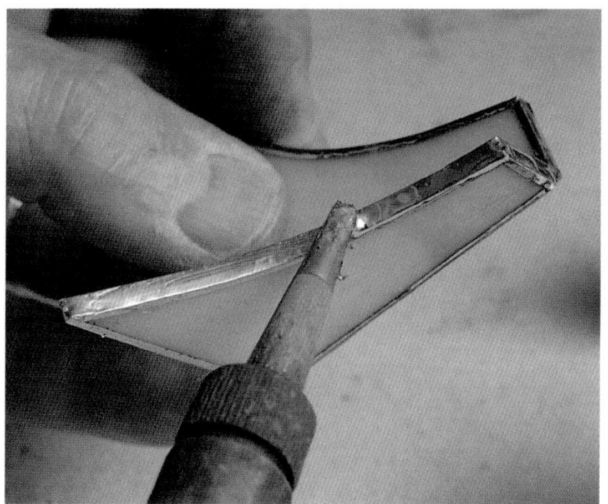

11 Check to be sure that all the copper is covered.

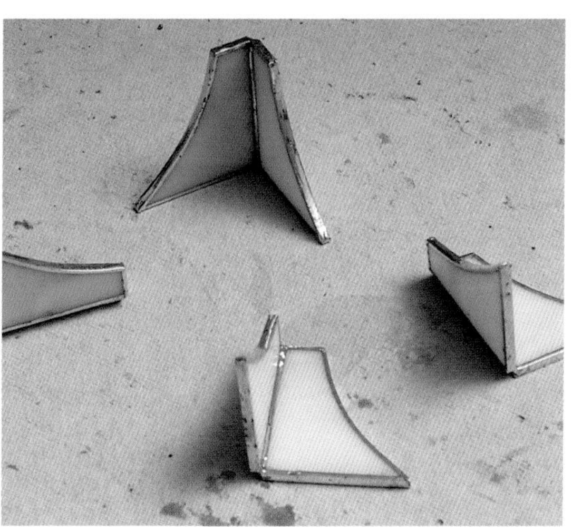

12 Then turn the box bottom upside down. Place a leg section on a box corner. It should be flush with the box sides.

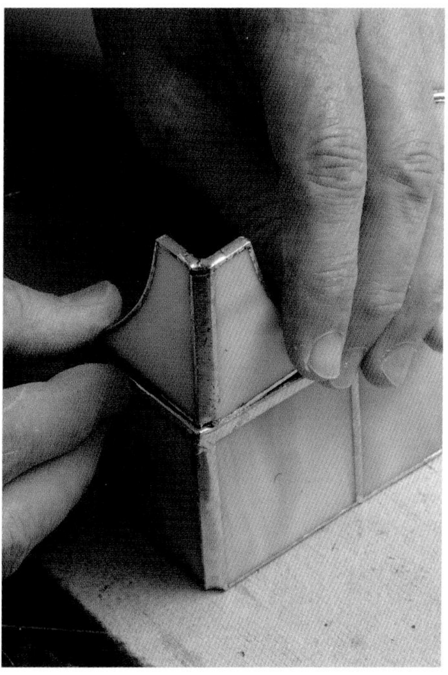

13 Flux and tack-solder.

14 Attach the three remaining legs in the same fashion. Bead the seams where the legs meet the box.

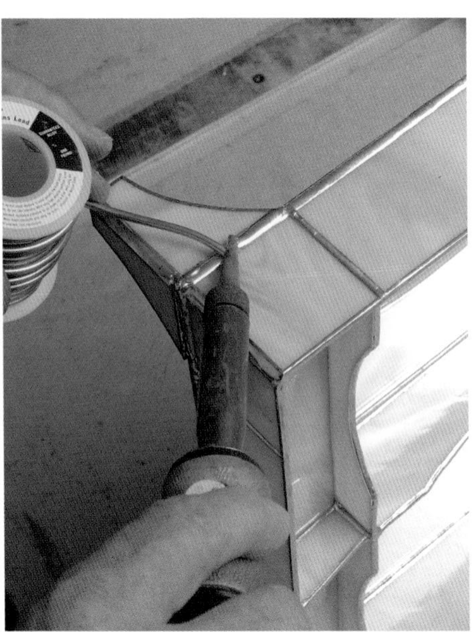

Hinging the Box

1 Each hinge on the box is made up of a 1/16-inch brass rod that fits into a 3/32-inch brass tube. (These items are commonly available in most stained glass shops.)

2 Mark the hinge tube at 2 1/2 inches from one end

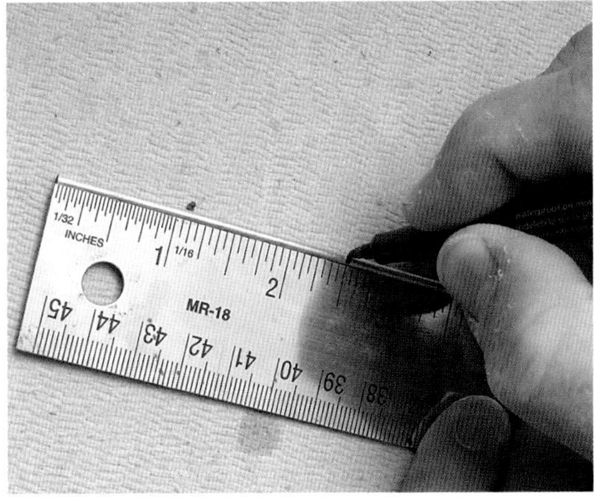

3 Take a small metal file and use a back-and-forth motion to scribe the tube several times. You will need to exert moderate pressure on the tube. Scribe the tube until you see a deep scratch.

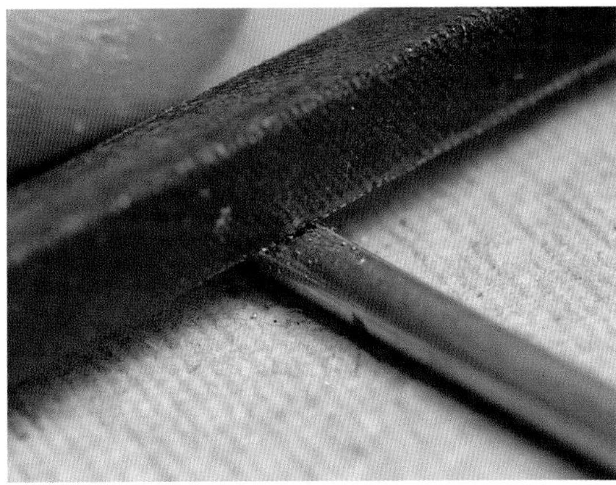

4 Place your thumbs on each side of the scratch and your fingers behind the scratch.

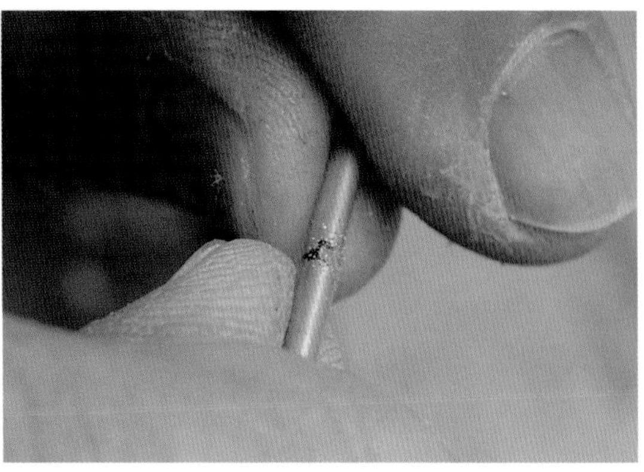

5 Push your thumbs out while pulling your index fingers in, causing the tube to bend and break. If this motion does not work, scribe deeper with the file.

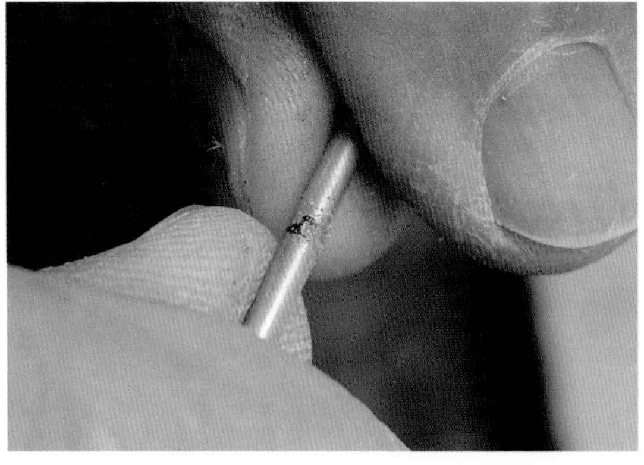

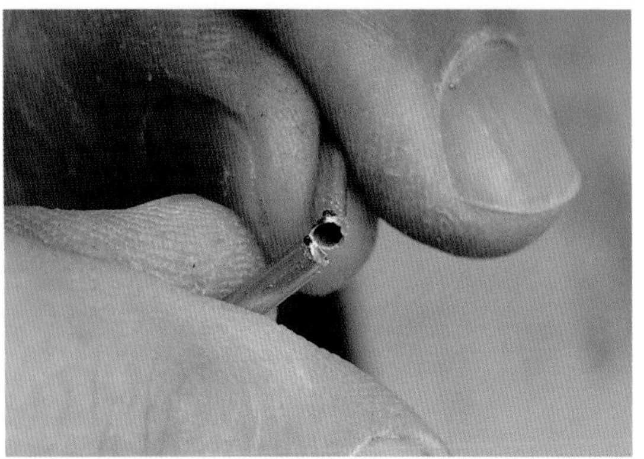

PRO TIP ✔

You cannot use wire cutters to cut the tube. Wire cutters will crush the end, and the rod will not fit.

6 Repeat these steps for the second hinge.

7 Cut two 4-inch lengths from the rod. Because these rods are solid, you will need to file deeper to break them. Use a back-and-forth sawing motion. If you have a hacksaw, that will also work.

8 Slip the rods into the tubes so one end protrudes 1/2 inch. Make a mark on each rod 1/2 inch from one end. With needle-nose pliers, bend the rod approximately 30 degrees at the mark. Repeat this step for the other rod.

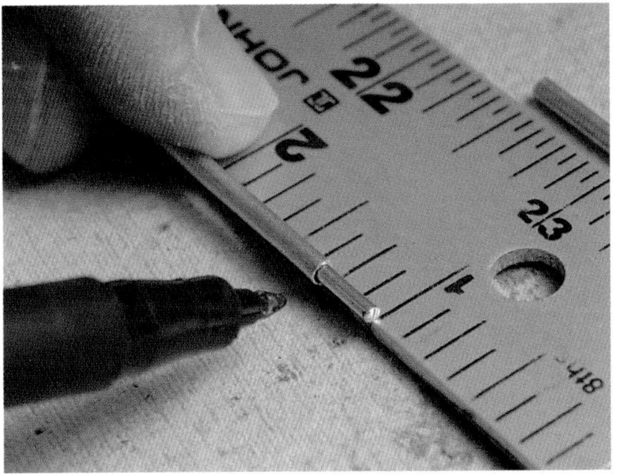

9 With wire cutters, cut off 1/4 inch of each rod, leaving about 1/4 inch.

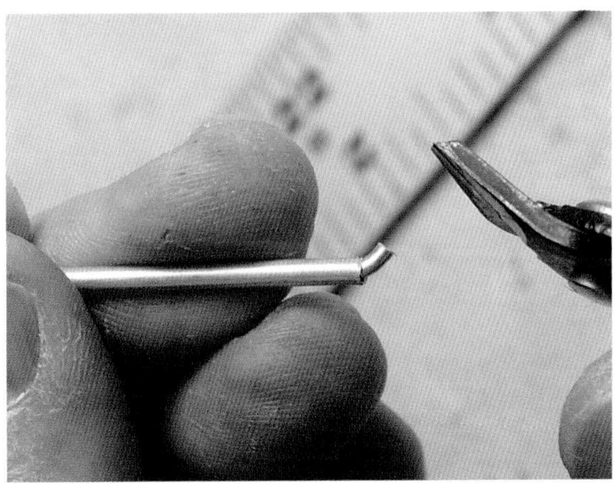

10 Pull the long end of the rod to snug the bend up to the tube. Holding the unit firmly, bend the long end of the rod to a 90-degree angle. Repeat these steps for the second hinge.

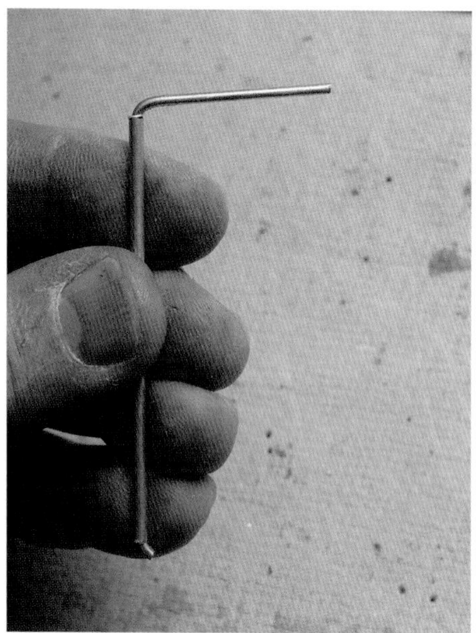

11 Set the box lid on the box bottom and position it as evenly as possible.

12 Hold a hinge at the back of the box so that the rod part is centered in the corner seam. Keep that position and mark the hinge and lid at any place along the tube part. This mark will enable you to line up the hinge properly when soldering.

13 Repeat these steps for the opposite side.

14 Set the box lid on the table and position the hinge accordingly so that the marks line up. The hinge will be flat on the table.

PRO TIP ✔

Take care not to get flux on the rod, because the flux might draw solder and cause the hinge parts to fuse together. If you inadvertently solder the hinge parts together, the hinge must be removed and discarded. Just create a new one.

15 Flux the tube part of the hinge and tack it to the lid. Solder along the tube, keeping the iron away from each end by about $^{1}/_{8}$ inch.

16 Repeat on the other side.

17 Check to see that the hinges are positioned so that the bent rods lie in the corner seams of the box.

18 Turn the lid upside down, flux the seam, and solder. Use only a thin coating of solder and work quickly to prevent solder from melting through to the top side.

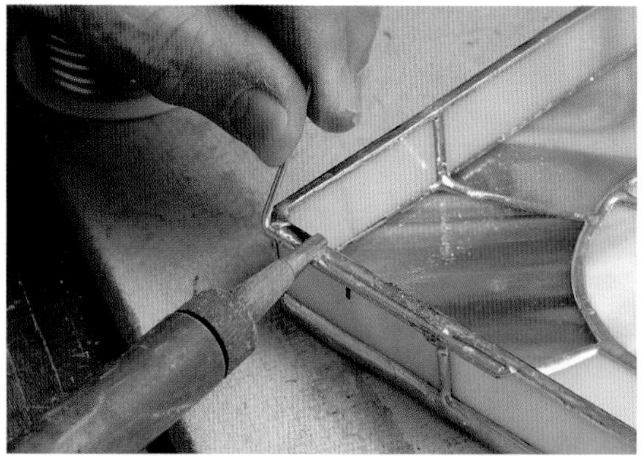

19 Position the lid on the box, ensuring that it is positioned evenly on all sides.

20 Flux the rod and tack-solder it to the corner seam. Hold the lid in place so it does not shift. Repeat this step on the other side.

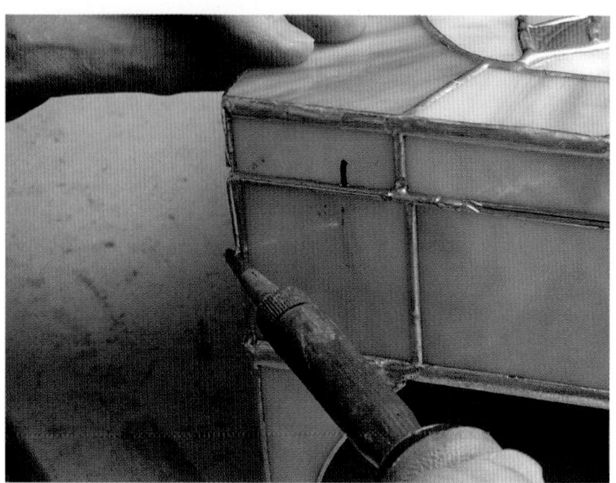

PRO TIPS ✔

Complete all the soldering of the top and bottom sections of the box before attaching the hinges. By even doing just a little touch-up, you run the risk of soldering the top and bottom together. This mistake can result in a major problem.

When soldering hinges, always tilt the seam you are working on away from the lid to avoid the same problem.

21 Open and close the lid to be sure it operates properly. The hinges should not touch the back of the box when the lid is open.

22 Hold the box so the corner is horizontal. Complete the soldering of both hinges in the box corners. Apply a little solder at a time so you don't remelt the solder where you tacked the hinge initially. This remelting could shift the hinge.

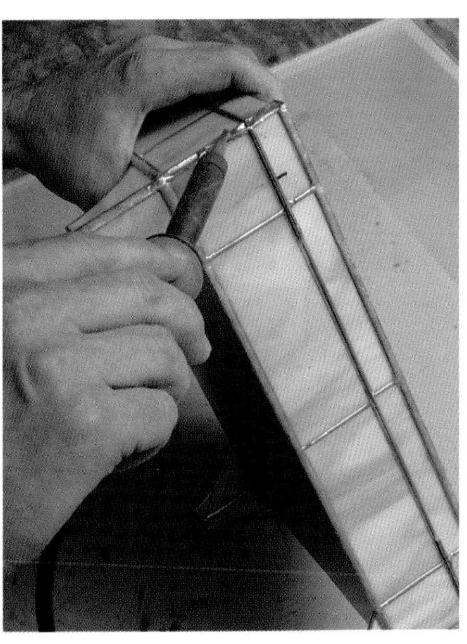

Attaching a Safety Chain

The last soldering step is to attach a safety chain. You will need about 15 inches of chain, but you should start with at least 18 inches.

1 Open the lid and support it on your wood blocks so that the hinges are not stressed.

2 Flux one or two links of the chain, and place it inside the box at the front vertical seam on the right side.

3 Solder one full link of chain to the bottom of the seam.

4 Pull on the chain to be sure the link is well attached. Then set the box upright and open the lid to about 100 degrees. (You do not really have to measure, just estimate the angle from the photo.)

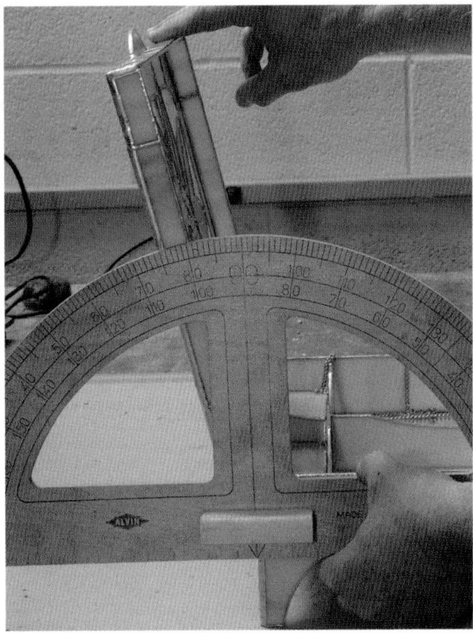

5 Hold the lid angle and pull the chain so that it meets the leaf point in the box lid as shown below. Hold that spot on the chain.

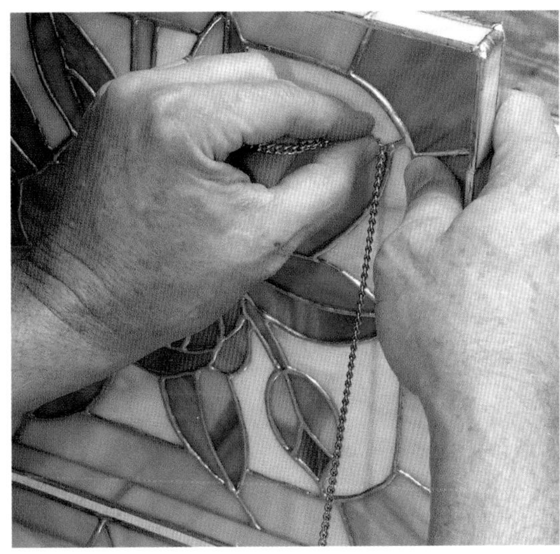

6 Set the lid on the blocks again and cut the chain at the correct spot.

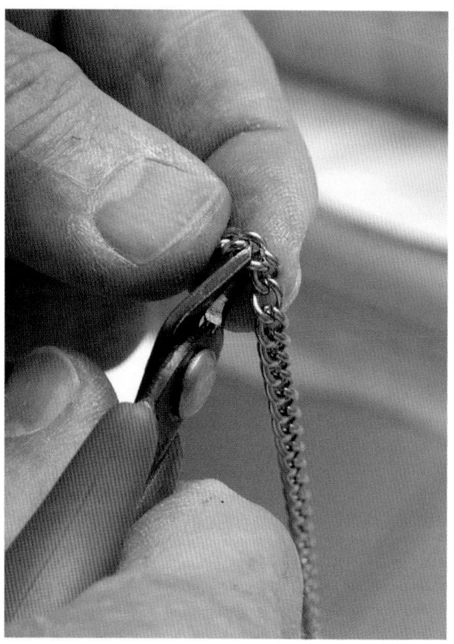

7 Carefully turn the box so the lid is upside down on the table. Place a wood block under the back edge of the box bottom. This position will allow some slack in the chain.

8 Hold the chain an inch or two from the soldering point to avoid burning yourself. Flux the chain and leaf point and solder one or two chain links to the lid. Pull to be sure the chain is secure.

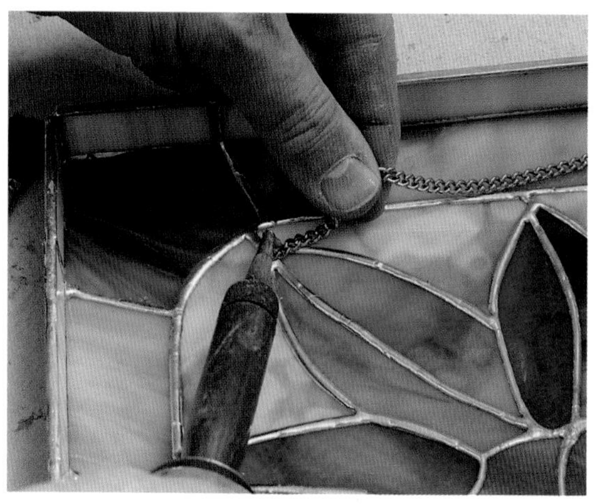

PRO TIP ✔

When soldering a chain or attaching other wires to any stained glass piece, rest your iron on the metal and allow the solder to melt and run down onto the connecting seam. By heating the metal in this way, a solid bond is formed.

9 Check to be sure the lid angle is to your liking and wipe off the flux at the hinges and chain.

Finishing the Project

Patina is a chemical that when applied to the solder seams will oxidize to various colors. The most common choices are black and copper. Black patina renders pretty much a jet black look. Copper turns to a "bright penny" finish. Now is the time for you to decide how you want to complete your box.

Leaving the box silver is fine if you like the look. If you used a lot of bright or light colors, black works nicely. Darker colors will be enhanced with copper.

The photos below should help. Remember: what you like best should be the deciding factor.

1 Give the box a thorough washing, rinsing, and drying to create a squeaky clean surface. A mild detergent is a good cleaner.

2 Spray on a flux/patina cleaner. Buff until dry. This step ensures a perfectly clean surface for applying the patina.

3 Shake the patina a few times with the cap on. Put on rubber gloves and carefully pour some patina onto a soft sponge.

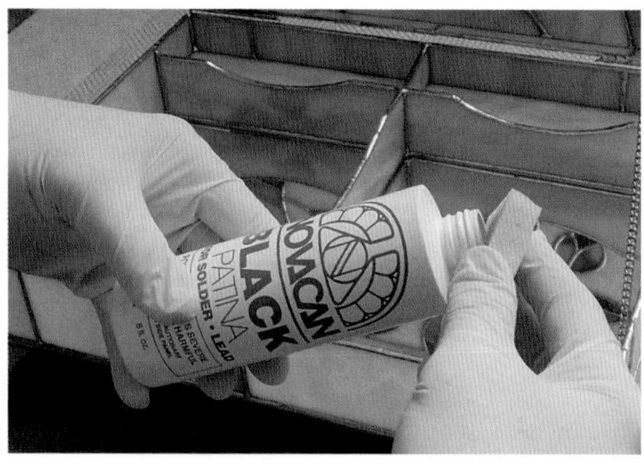

4 With a light back-and-forth scrubbing motion, rub patina over all the solder seams. Be generous with the patina.

PRO TIP ✔

Be cautious that you do not bump the chain too hard or let the lid drop as you wash, wax, or apply patina to the box.

5 Rinse off the majority of the patina. Then lightly go over the box with a clean sponge and patina cleaner. Be careful not to abrade the patina. Remember, it is only a surface coating. Rinse and dry thoroughly.

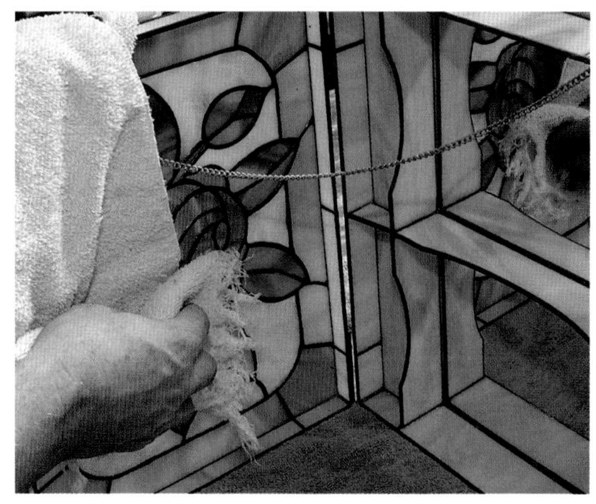

6 Spray liberally with flux/patina cleaner and buff dry.

7 Shake the finishing wax vigorously to blend it fully. Pour the liquid on the lid at a few spots, then spread it to all the solder seams with a soft cloth. Find a clean spot on the cloth and buff the wax to a bright shine.

8 Stand back and admire your masterpiece.

FINISHING THE PROJECT

- ❑ Clean project with a nontoxic all-purpose cleaner. Rinse and dry.
- ❑ Spray liberally with flux/patina cleaner. Buff until dry.
- ❑ Apply patina with soft sponge.
- ❑ Rinse off the patina.
- ❑ Spray liberally with flux/patina cleaner. Buff until dry.
- ❑ Apply finishing wax. Buff with soft cloth to bright shine.

Rose design

(Enlarge 220 percent)

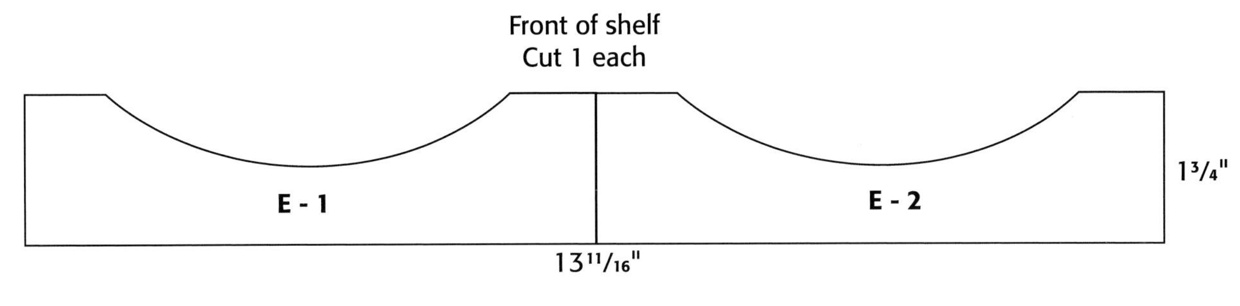

Lid lip
Front and back
Cut 2 each

D - 1
D - 2
D - 3
D - 4
3/4"
13 11/16"

Lid lip
Sides
Cut 2 each

C - 1
C - 2
C - 3
3/4"
10 11/16"

Sides
Cut 2 each

B - 1
B - 2
B - 3
2"
10 11/16"

Front and back
Cut 2 each

A - 1
A - 2
A - 3
A - 4
2"
13 11/16"

(Enlarge 220 percent)

Note: Box bottom 11" x 14"
For template, trace outline of box lid

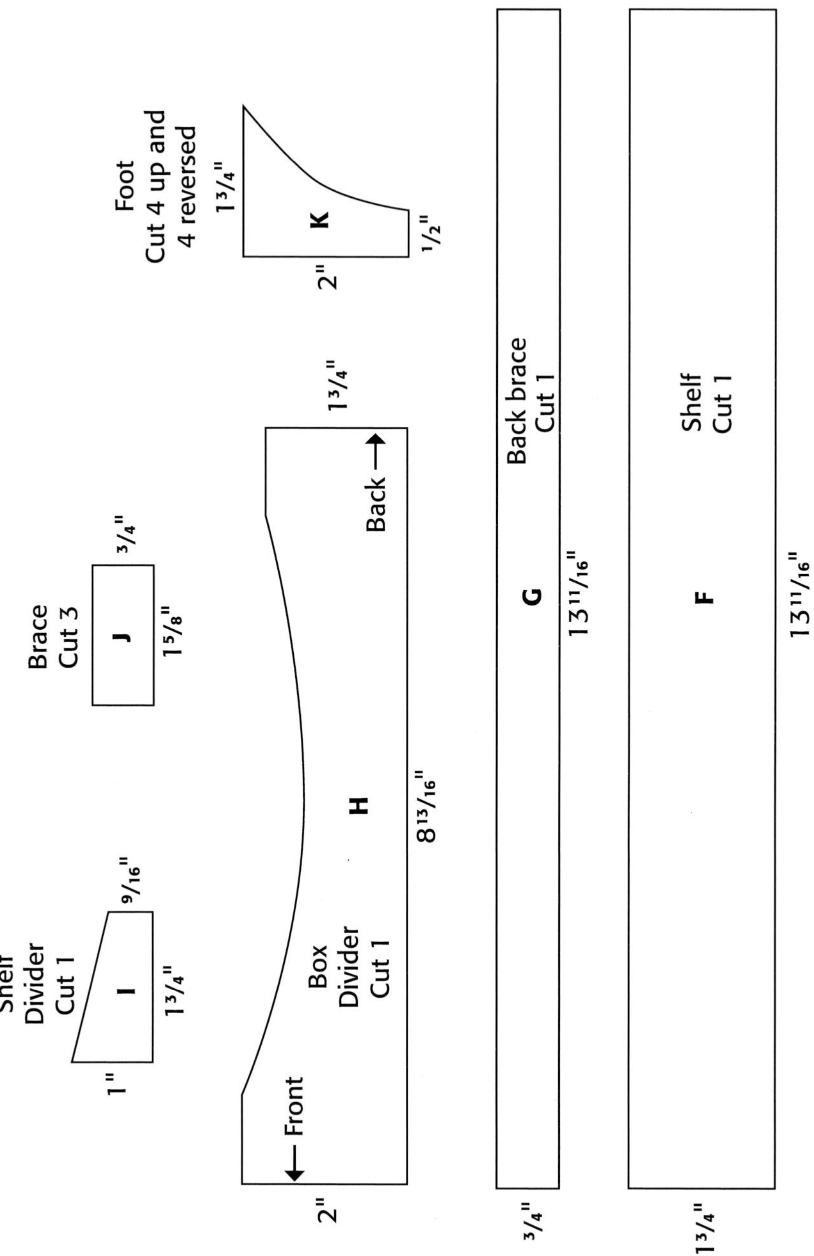

(Enlarge 220 percent)

Victorian Splendor design

(Enlarge 220 percent)

7 Basic Stained Glass Repair

A CRACKED PIECE OF GLASS IN A FINISHED project can happen for several reasons. However, it is not something that should be met with a great deal of concern. Many years ago, my friend John, who was a student with us back in the late 1980s, completed a large Tiffany-style lamp. He had spent many hours making a very nice shade. I was stunned when he called in a panic telling me his lamp was broken. I was envisioning a dropped and smashed pile of rubble. After questioning him, I found out that only one piece was cracked. John came in that day for a repair lesson, and his shade was as good as new in 30 minutes.

If you should have the misfortune of discovering a cracked piece or two in your finished jewelry box, you will find that it is not too hard to remedy.

1 First, you will want to remove the lid from the box. Open the box and lay the lid upside down on the work surface. Support the box bottom with a block.

2 Flux the spot where the safety chain is connected to the lid. Place your iron on the solder. As the solder melts, pull the chain loose from its connection.

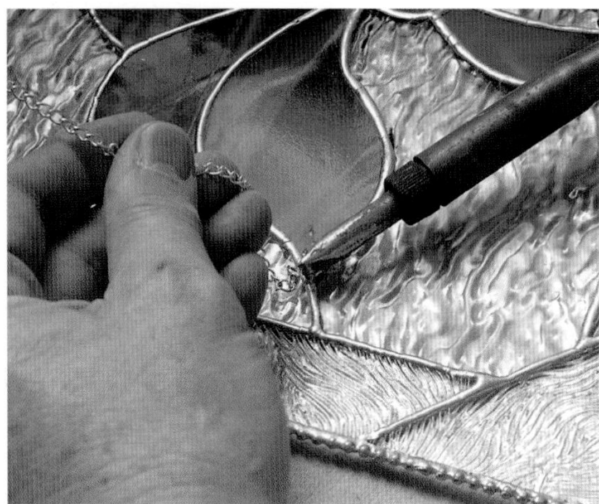

3 Set the box upright.

4 Flux the hinge rod that is soldered in one of the corners. Melt the solder holding the rod and, as it melts, push the lid back and away so the rod is no longer touching the box.

5 Repeat for the hinge on the other side of the box.

6 Lay the lid flat and make several scores on the broken piece. Initial scores should be in a tic-tac-toe design. Be sure scores are also made in the corners of the piece. (Scoring is indicated here by marked lines.)

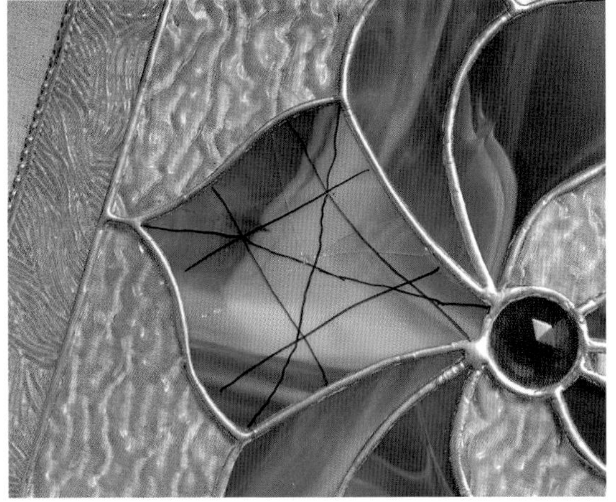

7 Turn the lid over and tilt it to one side. Using the brass screw on the cutter, tap in the center of each score, causing the glass to crack. (Note: you are tapping on the back of the lid.) Continue tapping on the center pieces until they fall out.

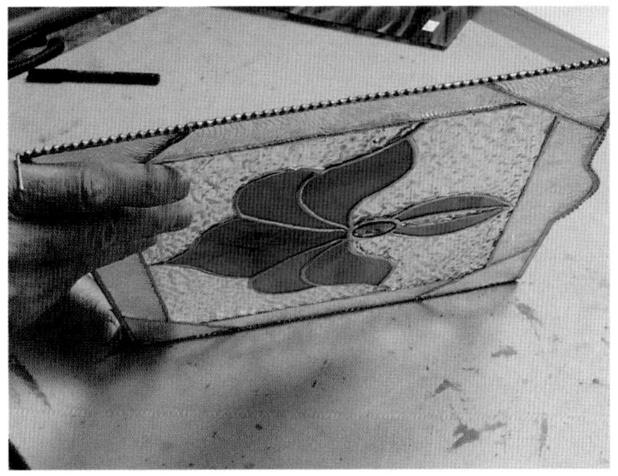

8 Clean up the debris.

9 Using needle-nose pliers, take hold of any remaining piece and melt the solder that is holding that piece in. Move the iron back and forth and, as the solder melts, gently pull the piece loose.

10 Remove all of the other pieces the same way.

11 Look closely at the opening and determine where the foil from the broken piece is located. Use your iron to melt that area and separate the seam. Use your needle-nose pliers to pull away one end of the foil from the molten solder.

12 Secure the foil end in the pliers and melt the solder at that area. As the solder melts, gently pull away the foil from the seam. Continue in this fashion until you have removed all the foil from the broken piece of glass.

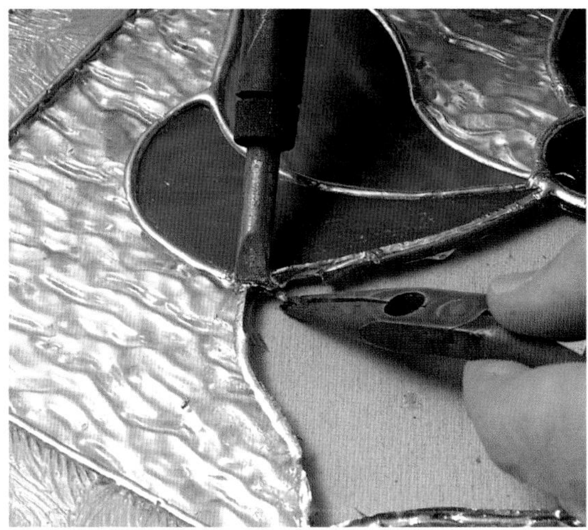

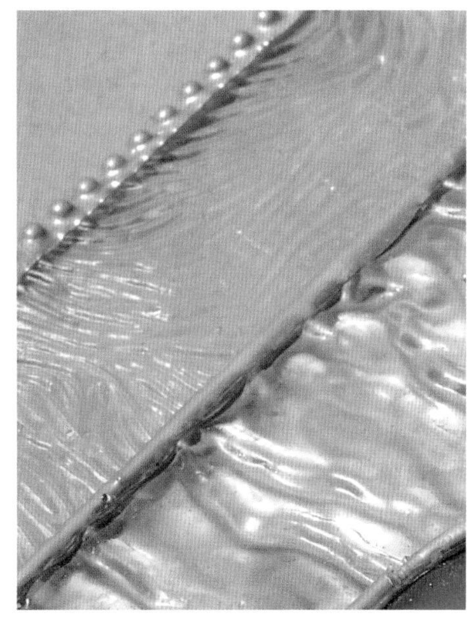

13 Tilt the lid up an inch or two and flux the inside opening. Melt off the remaining solder, letting it drop to the surface. The opening should have only a thin coating of solder left.

14 Place a piece of replacement glass on the work surface. Move the lid until it lines up with a section of glass you want to use for the repair.

15 Trace the shape onto the new glass.

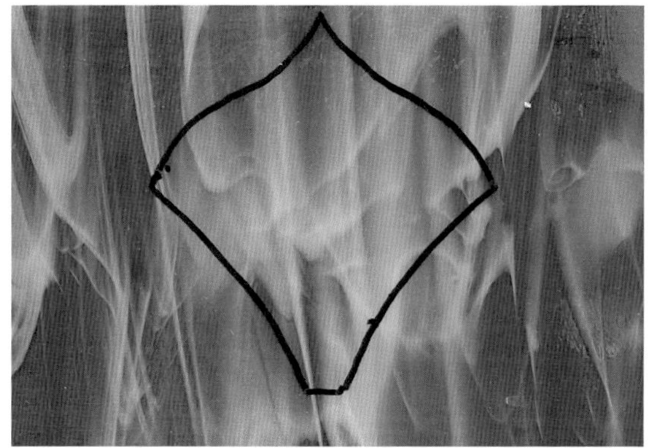

16 Cut the new glass. If you cut through the center of the marker lines, you should have an accurate replacement piece.

17 Check for fit and adjust as needed. The piece should be a little loose to accommodate the foil. Wash the piece and foil it.

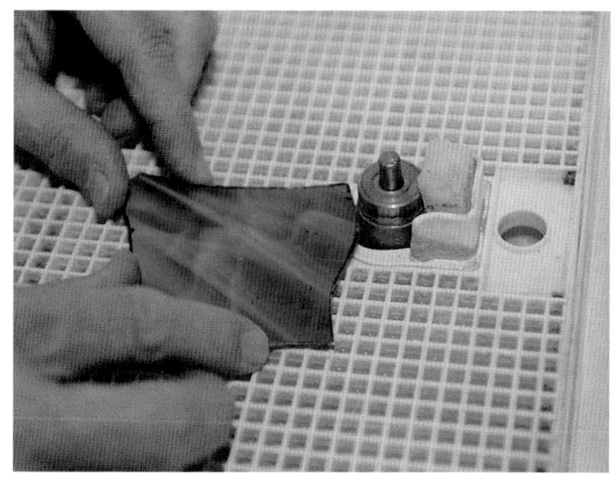

18 Flux the opening and newly foiled replacement piece.

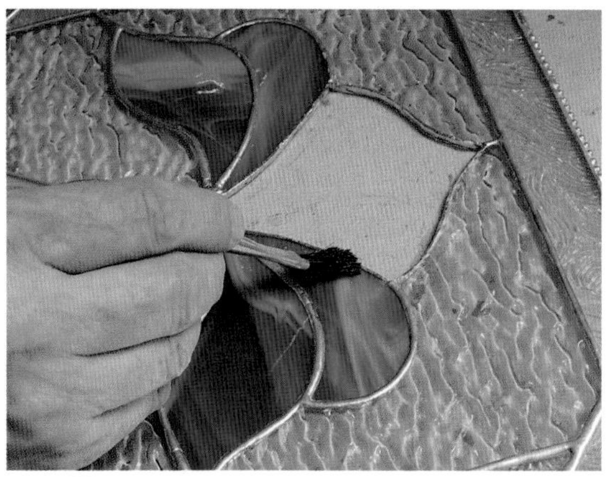

19 Pull the lid over the table edge so you can hold the new piece. Insert it now.

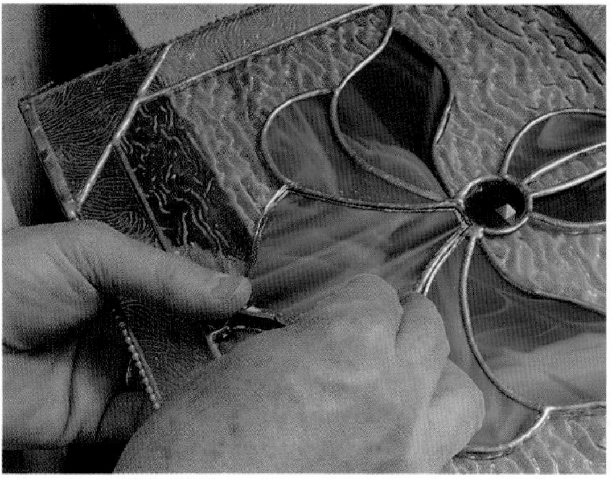

20 Tack-solder at several points.

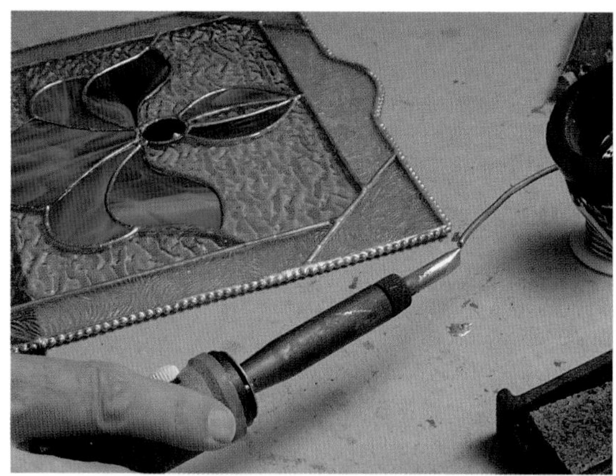

21 Finish soldering, front and back.

22 Reattach the hinge legs and safety chain. Do a final cleaning and finishing.

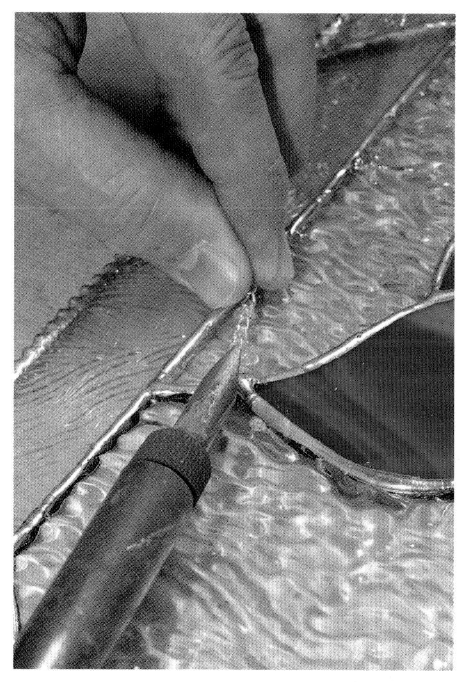

8

Stained Glass Box Gallery

Victorian Splendor
Designed and fabricated by Nan Maund

Victorian Wings
Rainbow Vision Stained Glass
This box is featured in *Beyond Basic Stained Glass Making* (Stackpole Books, 2007).

Rose (alternate colors)
Rainbow Vision Stained Glass

Southwest Hex
Designed and fabricated by Lynn Haunstein

Angled Iris
Rainbow Vision Stained Glass

Web of Intrigue
Designed and fabricated by Lee Summer
This box features a circular piece of agate that has been foiled and soldered into the lid.

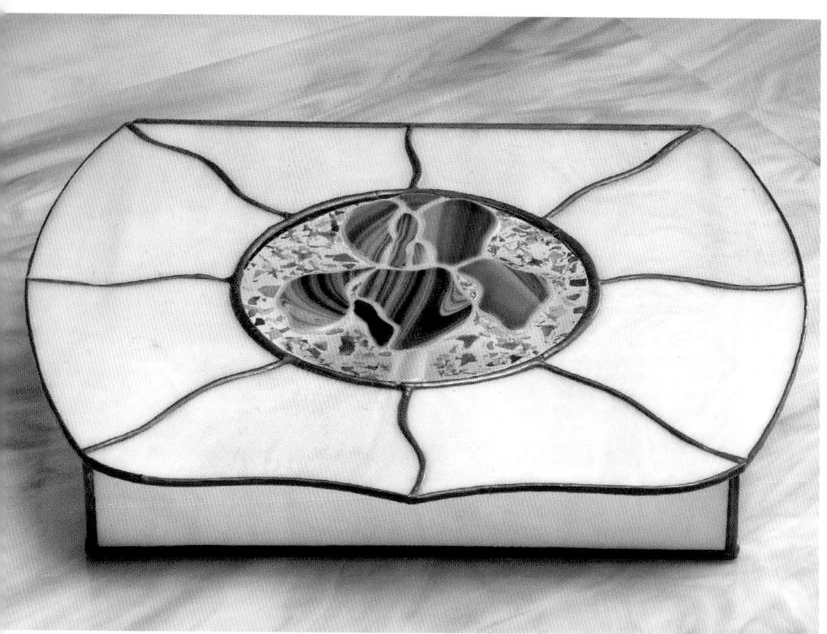

Fused Iris

Rainbow Vision Stained Glass

This box lid has a fused circular medallion as its focal point.

Fluttering Hummingbird

Rainbow Vision Stained Glass

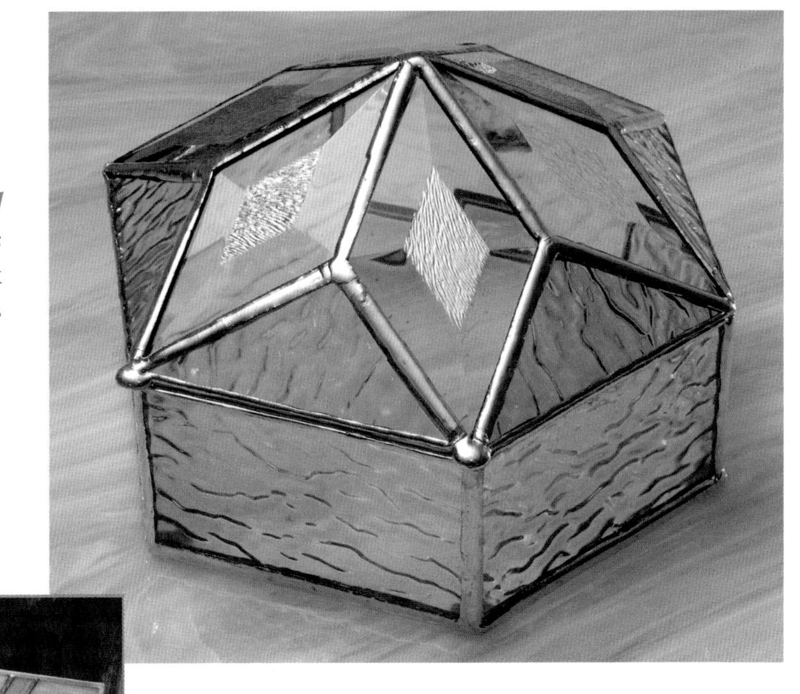

Dichroic Pyramid

Rainbow Vision Stained Glass

This box lid features six dichroic diamond bevels soldered in three dimensions.

Splendid Rainbow

Rainbow Vision Stained Glass

This box features a lower drawer and a sectional top opening. It was constructed using a $^{1}/_{8}$-inch brass channel.

Monogram Box

Rainbow Vision Stained Glass

This box features colorful Van Gogh glass and colored mirror.

Trio of Diamonds

Rainbow Vision Stained Glass

The lid of this box design is slightly three dimensional as a result of the angle formed by joining three 3 by 5-inch diamond bevels. Note that the box sides are angled at the top as well to accommodate the irregular shape of the lid.

additional box patterns

The patterns on the following pages are included to provide several different options for making glass boxes. Assuming you've finished the featured box to your satisfaction, you should find these new options to be considerably easier. For additional box designs and their detailed instructions, please visit www.rainbowvisionsg.com. *Enlarge the following patterns to 250 percent.*

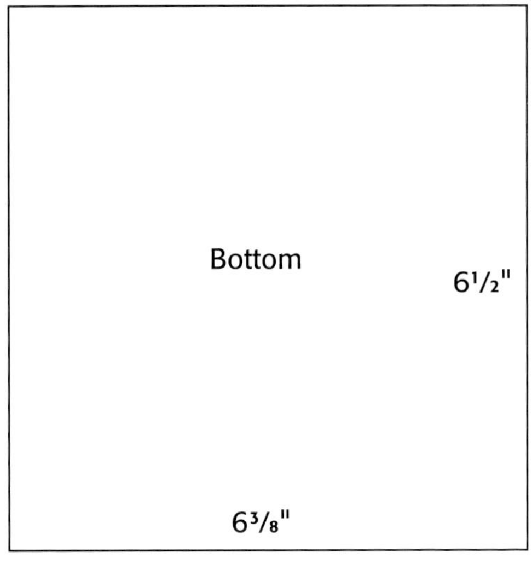

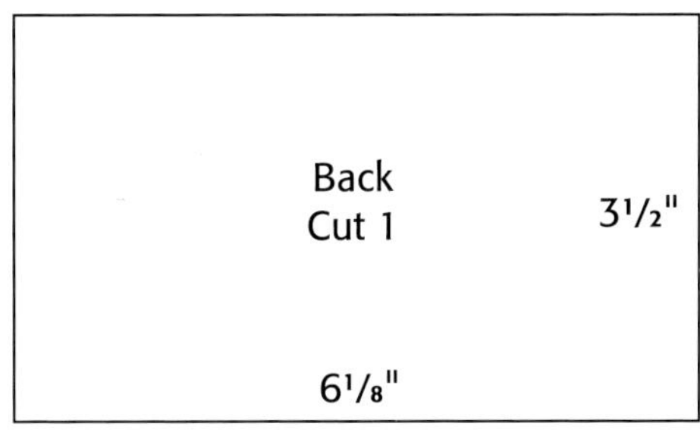

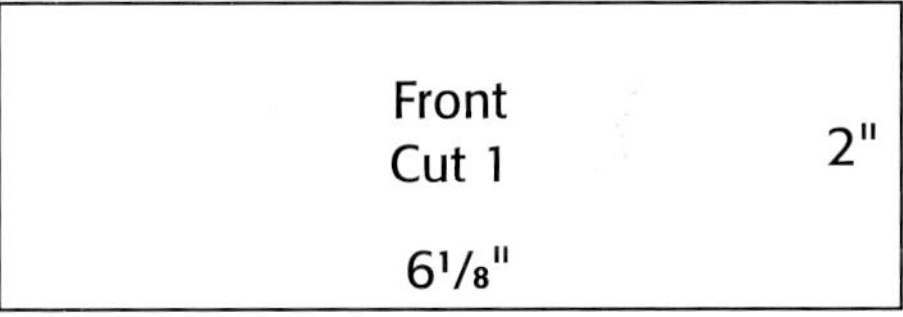

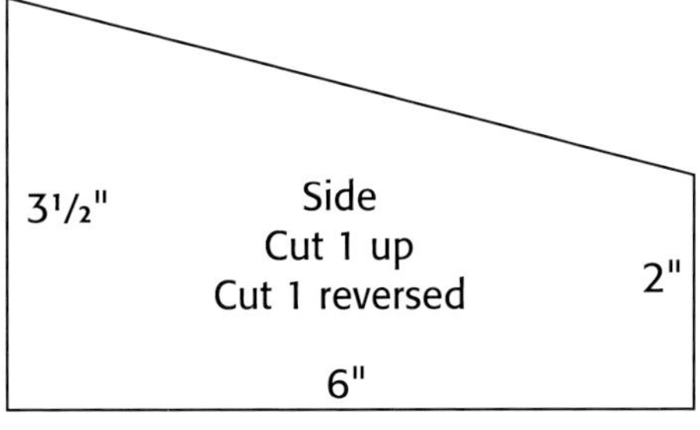

Angled Iris

Fused Iris

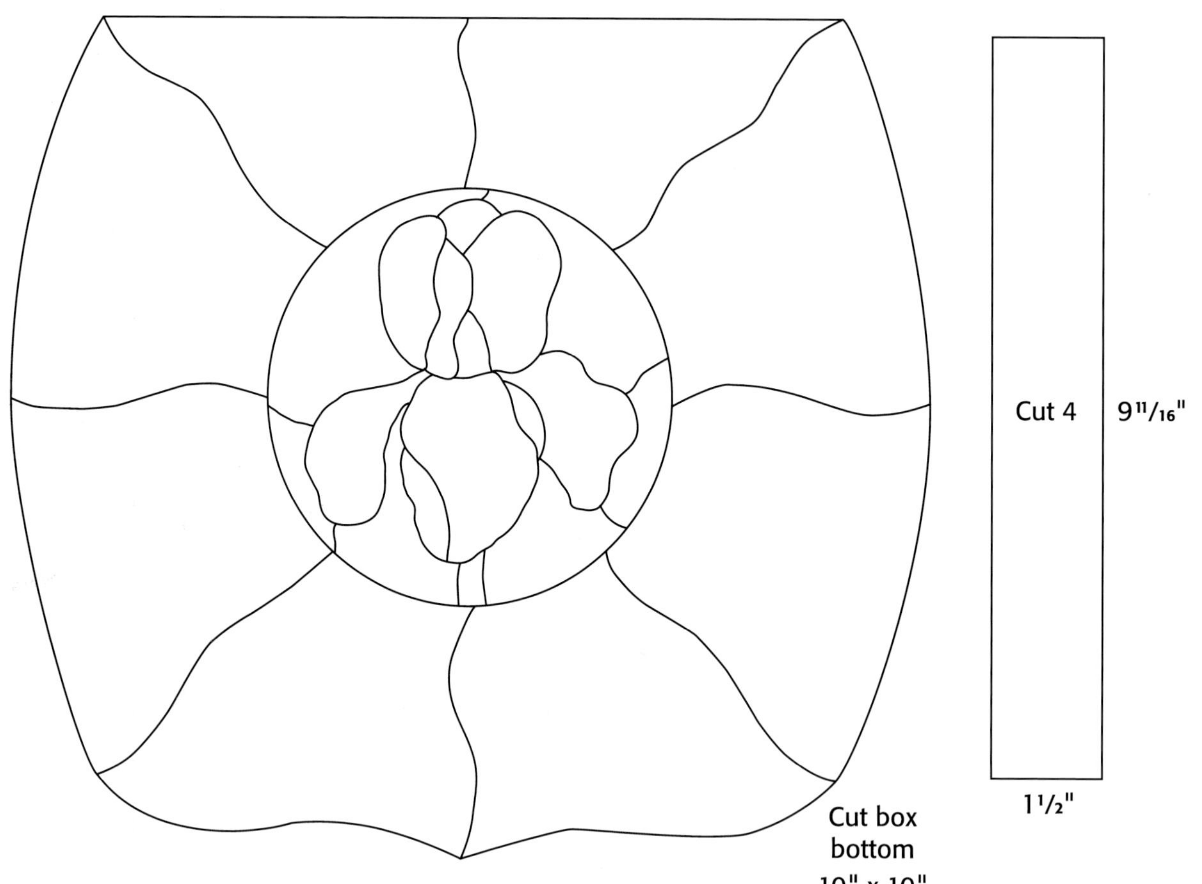

Fluttering Hummingbird

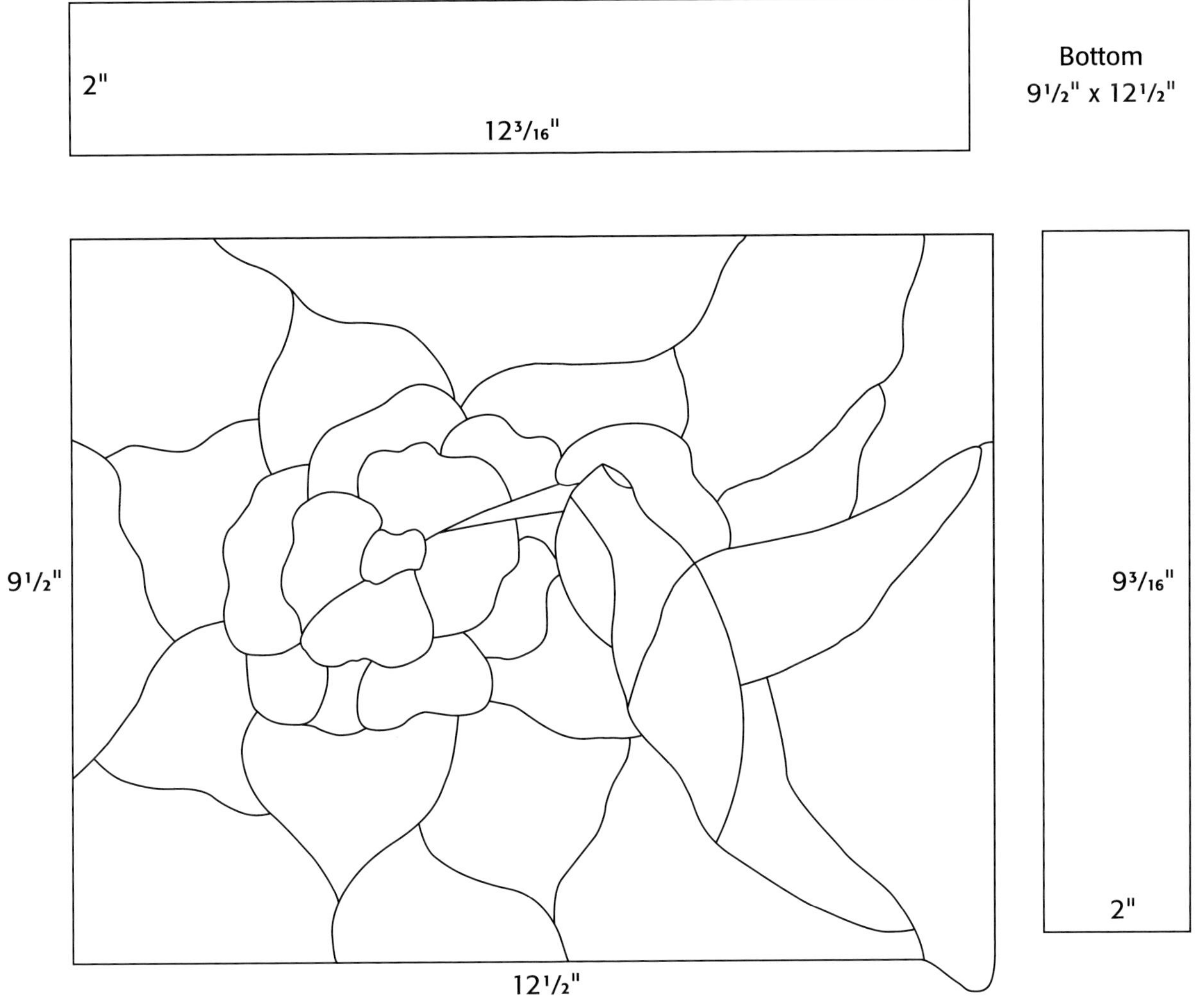

Monogram Box

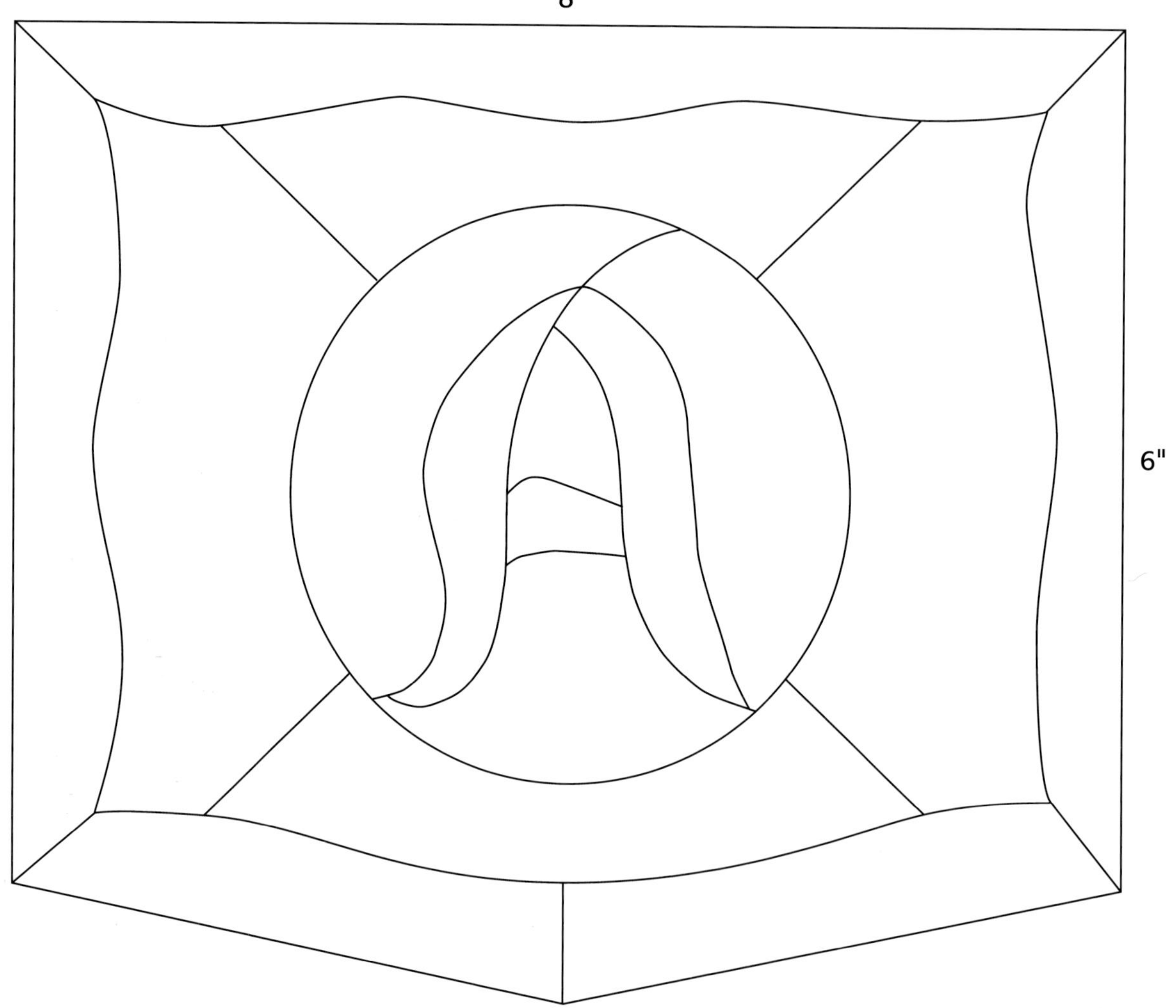

Front and back $1^1/_2$" x $7^{11}/_{16}$"
Sides $1^1/_2$" x $5^{11}/_{16}$"
Bottom 6" x 8"

For additional letters and styles, see *Classic Alphabets* (Wardell Publications, 1987).

resources

Books

Sibbett, Ed. *Easy to Make Stained Glass Boxes.* Mineola, NY. Dover Publications, 1984.

Stewart, Christine. *Bead Chain Boxes Mirrors and Displays.* Olympia, WA: CKE Publishing, 2005.

Wardell, Randy. *Stained Glass Boxes.* Fort Lauderdale, FL: Wardell Publications, 1989.

Werderits, Margaret. *Contemporary Glass Boxes.* Ada, MI: Stained Glass News Publishing, 2002.

Online

Glastar Corp.
20721 Marilla Street
Chatsworth, CA 91311
800-423-5635
www.glastar.com
Manufacturer of glass grinders and other stained glass tools. This site includes lots of glass-related topics.

Inland Craft Products, Co.
32052 Edward Drive
Madison Heights, MI 48071
800-521-8428
www.inlandcraft.com
Carries glass grinders and other equipment used in stained glass. Also includes a handy state-by-state locator of stained glass supply stores.

Kokomo Opalescent Glass
1310 S. Market Street
Kokomo, IN 46904-2265
765-457-8136
www.kog.com
The oldest glass manufacturer in the country, established in 1888. Take a virtual tour of the factory, click on their sample set, and see products from their hot glass studio.

Rainbow Vision Stained Glass
3105 Walnut Street
Harrisburg, PA 17109
800-762-9309
www.rainbowvisionsg.com
Contains information about all things stained glass; equipment and materials available for purchase.

Retailers of Art Glass and Supplies (RAGS)
www.stainedglassretailers.com
A nonprofit organization of owners of retail stores selling stained glass supplies around the world. Includes good information about the craft, as well as listings of supplier locations.

Spectrum Glass
24105 Sno-Woodinville Road
Woodinville, WA 98072
425-483-6699
www.spectrumglass.com
This site is loaded with technical information, sample colors, free patterns, and much more.

Uroboros Glass
2139 North Kerby Avenue
Portland, OR 97227
503-284-4900
www.uroboros.com
This site includes details about the factory and glass samples.

Wissmach Glass, Co.
420 Stephen Street
Paden City, WV 26159
304-337-2253
www.wissmachglass.com
This site has factory information, glass samples, and a gallery.

Youghiogheny Glass
900 West Crawford Avenue
Connellsville, PA 15425
724-628-0332
www.youghioghenyglass.com
Established in 1978, this company specializes in Tiffany reproduction glass. This site includes sample sets, gallery, and factory information.